Kopiervorlagen für den Englischunterricht

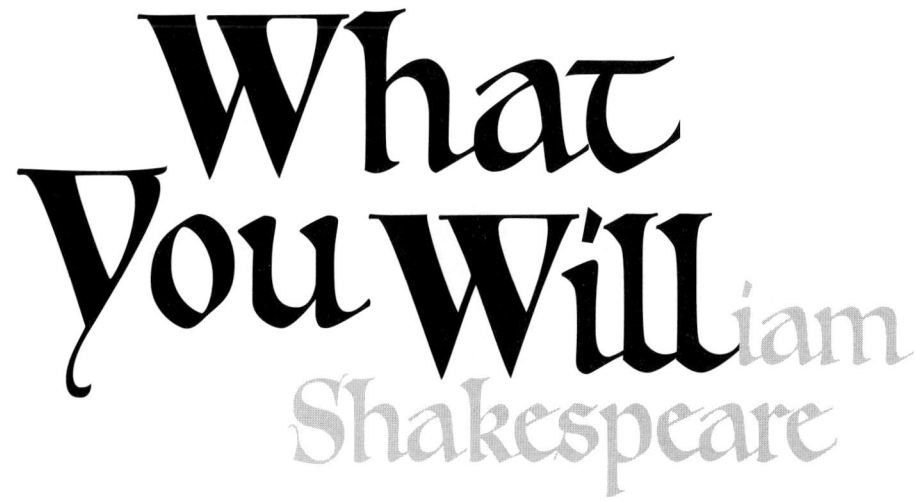

What You William Shakespeare

W0197524

Cornelsen

Susanne Schroeder-Thürauf (Hrsg.),
Horst Mühlmann, Philip Town,
Harald Weißling, Bob Yareham

What You Will: Shakespeare

In Zusammenarbeit mit der Verlagsredaktion
Ingrid von der Felsen-Ferguson, Bettina Schaschke (Assistenz)

Illustrationen
Holger Lipschütz

Umschlag
Knut Waisznor

Gestaltung und technische Umsetzung
Fred-Michael Sauer

 http://www.cornelsen.de

1. Auflage   Druck 4 3 2 1   Jahr 06 05 04 03

© 2003 Cornelsen Verlag, Berlin

Druck: CS-Druck CornelsenStürtz, Berlin

ISBN 3-464-37113-1

Bestellnummer 371131

Gedruckt auf Recyclingpapier, hergestellt aus 100 % Altpapier.

CONTENTS

Language Workshop

What Else?

Notes

Thou classroom locked

Word-plagued young people,

Thou text obsessed

Text-composing mistresses and masters,

Let us on your imaginary forces work,

Follow me on my Shakespeare trail.

What about a day in London?

Meet me on the Verona balcony.

Let my plays draw back the curtains

of history,

Come – join the party on stage!

Hear, hear!!

So, don't plague us even more!

Not again??

With some original suggestions, I hope!

Shall we??

Why read this old stuff after 400 years?

William Who?

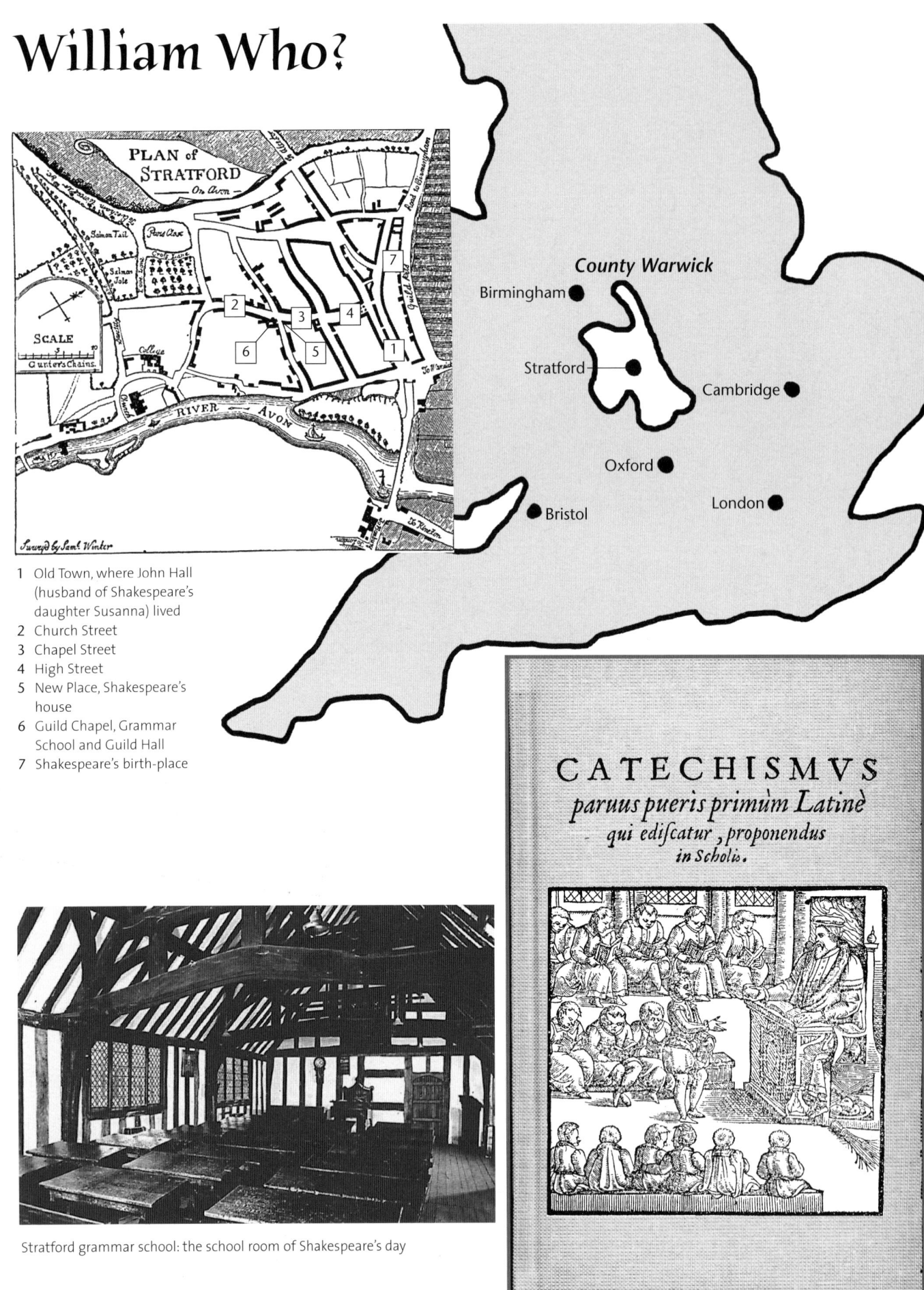

1 Old Town, where John Hall (husband of Shakespeare's daughter Susanna) lived
2 Church Street
3 Chapel Street
4 High Street
5 New Place, Shakespeare's house
6 Guild Chapel, Grammar School and Guild Hall
7 Shakespeare's birth-place

Stratford grammar school: the school room of Shakespeare's day

At grammar school: the pupils mainly learned to read, write and speak Latin and study classical literature.

Anne Hathaway was the daughter of a farmer who lived near Stratford. She was born in 1556 and gave William three children:
Susan, born 5 months after their marriage (1582);
Hamnet and Judith (twins: 1585).

From the church register of Holy Trinity Church in Stratford: Baby Will is supposed to have been born three days before his baptism: See the line with XXX.

An exciting discovery was made in 2001 over the supposed home of Shakespeare's mother. The house that Will's mother, Mary Arden, lived in before she married John Shakespeare and moved to Stratford was thought to have been the attractive Tudor farmhouse at Wilmcote. However, it has been discovered that Mary Arden in fact owned *Glebe Farm*, a property very close by in the same village. *Glebe Farm* is actually in the ownership of the National Trust and will now assume the Arden name. The 'old' *Mary Arden's House* will now be known as *Palmer's Farm*.

In 1564 John Shakespeare was a rising man. Born about 1529, the son of a small tenant farmer in Snitterfield, near Stratford-upon-Avon, John became a successful glover occupying a comfortable house in Henley Street, Stratford, and owning another in Greenhill Street. He was one of the senior figures in Stratford's town council.

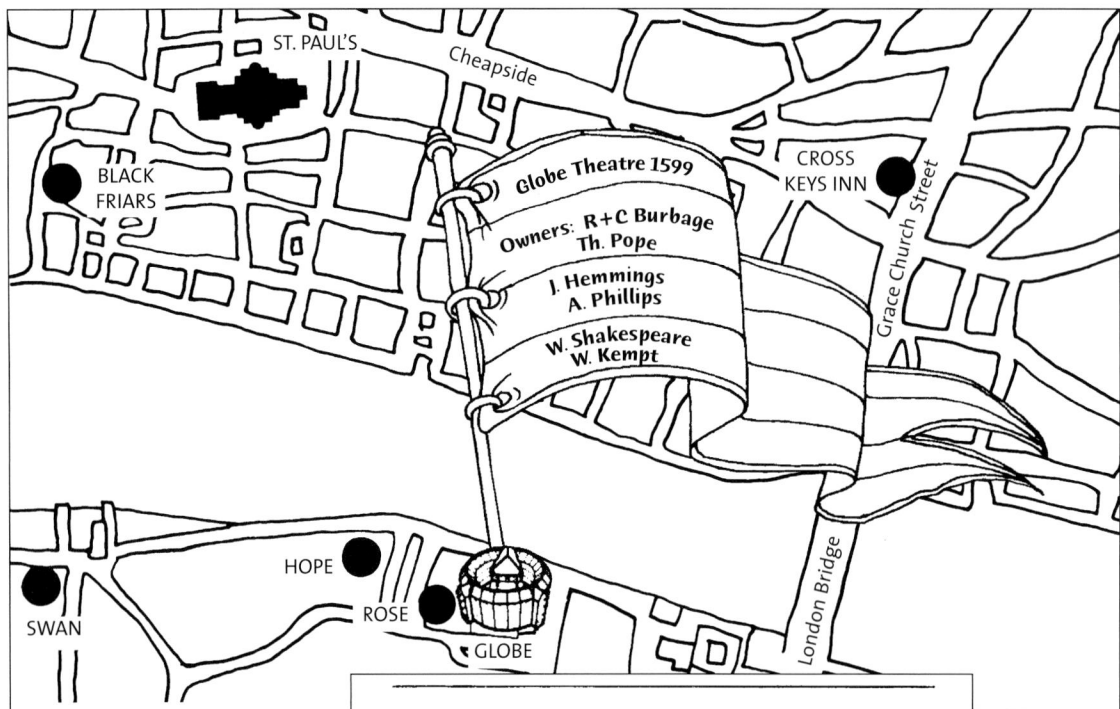

In Shakespeare's day a real gentleman not only needed money but also a *coat of arms* to show that his family was old and respected. William had one made for his father in 1596.

The Workes of William Shakespeare,

containing all his Comedies, Histories, and Tragedies: Truely set forth, according to their first ORIGINALL.

The Names of the Principall Actors
in all these Playes.

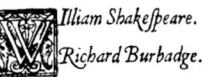

William Shakespeare.	Samuel Gilburne.
Richard Burbadge.	Robert Armin.
John Hemmings.	William Ostler.
Augustine Phillips	Nathan Field.
William Kempt.	John Underwood.
Thomas Poope.	Nicholas Tooley.
George Bryan.	William Ecclestone.
Henry Condell.	Joseph Taylor.
William Slye.	Robert Benfield.
Richard Cowly.	Robert Goughe.
John Lowine.	Richard Robinson.
Samuell Crosse.	John Shancke.
Alexander Cooke.	John Rice.

The list of actors of the *First-Folio*-Issue, 1623

How William spent the nine years after the birth of his twins is not known. The next place we hear of him is the big city above.

New Place, Stratford's second largest house, bought by W. Shakespeare in 1597

After his death on 23rd April 1616 Shakespeare was buried at Holy Trinity Church, Stratford.

William Who?

Last name: _____

First name: _____

Place of birth: _____

_____
street   town

_____
county   country

Date of birth: _____

Mother: _____

Mother's family: _____

Father: _____

Father's profession: _____

School: _____

Marriage: _____

Possible reason
for marriage: _____

Children: _____

Place of residence
from 1585 – 1594: _____

Place of residence
in 1594: _____

Profession from
1594 on: _____

Coat of arms: _____

Additional
profession in 1599: _____

Financial situation
in later life: _____

Date of death: _____

Grave: _____

GOOD FREND FOR IESUS SAKE FORBEARE,
TO DIGG THE DUST ENCLOSED HEARE;
BLEST BE Ẏ MAN Ẏ SPARES HES STONES,
AND CVRST BE HE Ẏ MOVES MY BONES.

Shakespeare's tombstone in Holy Trinity Church,
Stratford-upon-Avon

Engraving by William Marshall, 1640

- Have a look at the pictures and texts on p. 6–9. They give you all the information you need to complete the data form about Shakespeare.

- Write a short biography of William Shakespeare adding details you might find in books, films, articles, encyclopaedias, etc.

"By me William Shakespeare"
Will's signature, 25th March, 1616

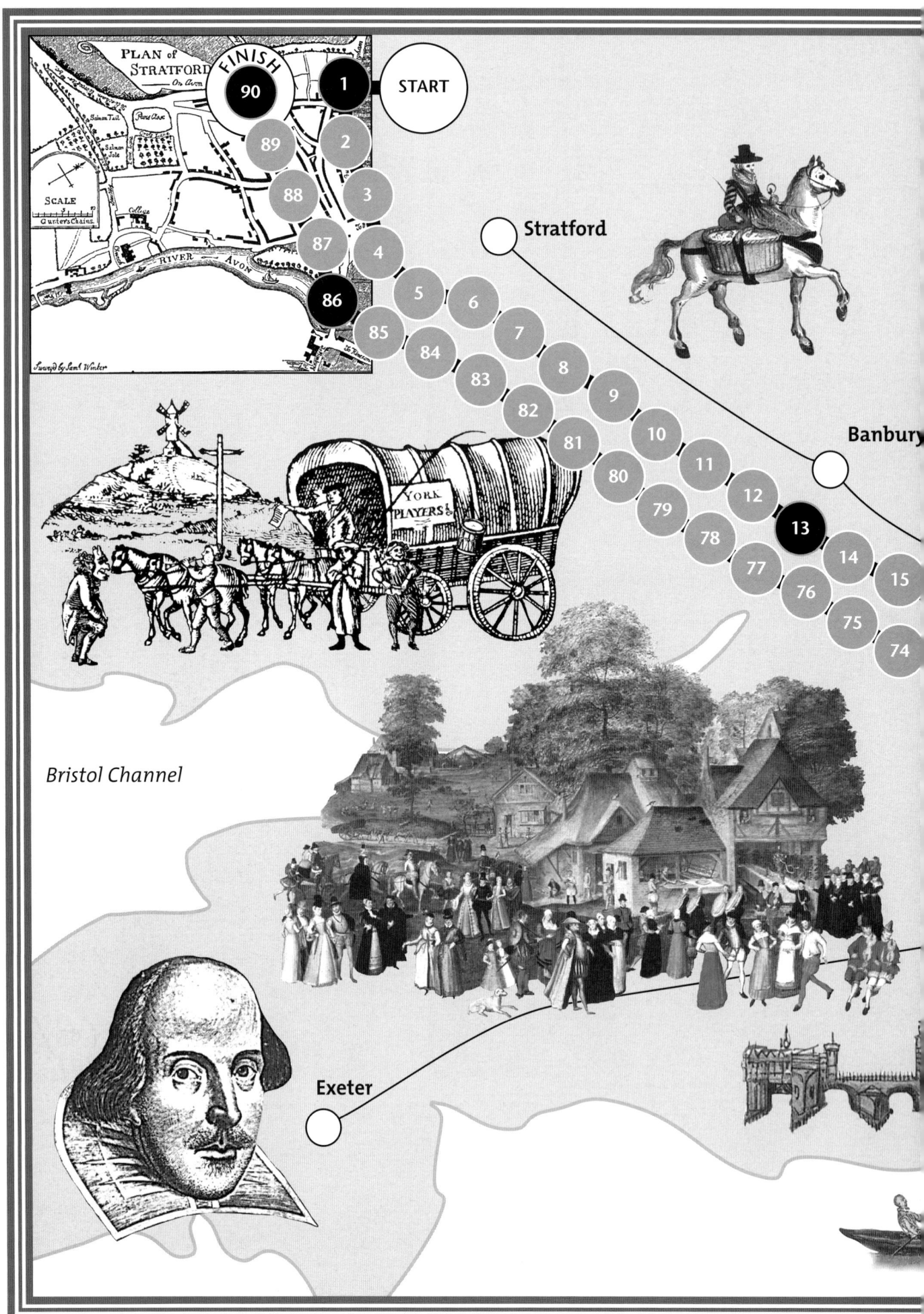

START

FINISH

90

1

2

3

4

5

6

7

8

9

10

11

12

13

14

15

74

75

76

77

78

79

80

81

82

83

84

85

86

87

88

89

Stratford

Banbury

Bristol Channel

Exeter

PLAN of STRATFORD On Avon

RIVER AVON

SCALE
Gunters Chain

YORK PLAYERS &

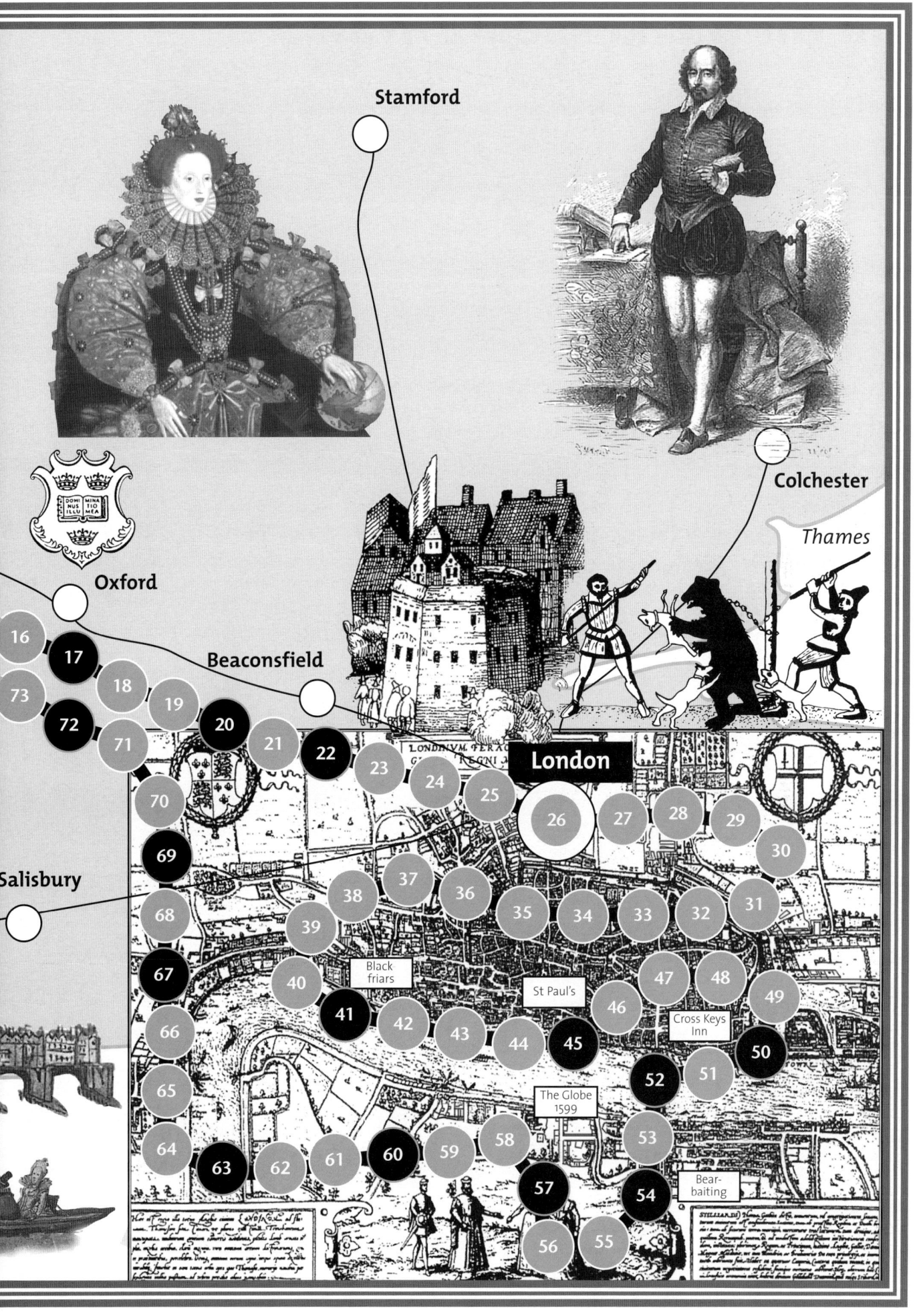

Stamford

Colchester

Thames

Oxford

16
17
73
18
72
71
19
20
21
22
23
24
25

Beaconsfield

LONDINVM FERAC
GE REGNI

London

26
27
28
29
30

70

69

37
36
35
34
33
32
31

Salisbury

68
38
39

67
40
Black friars
St Paul's
47
48
49
46
66
41
42
43
44
45
Cross Keys Inn
50
52
51
65
The Globe 1599
53
64
63
62
61
60
59
58
57
54
Bear-baiting
56
55

STILLIARDS

On the Shakespeare Trail

(START) → Shakespeare was probably 23 when he first set off for London.

START → **So collect at least 23 points before you can set off on your journey: In the first round each player has five throws of the dice.**

1 Here is *Shakespeare's birthplace:*
→ **When you've got 23 points (or more) go to ①.**

13 At the beginning of his professional career Shakespeare would have taken four days to walk from Stratford to London, with a first overnight stop at **Banbury.**

ᴀ ʜᴏʀsᴇ! ᴀ ʜᴏʀsᴇ! ᴍʏ ᴋɪɴɢᴅᴏᴍ ꜰᴏʀ ᴀ ʜᴏʀsᴇ! (Richard III)
→ **If you end up in *Banbury*, miss a turn.**

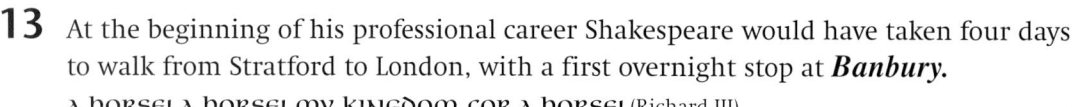

17 Next overnight stop: **Oxford.** Even in later years when he travelled by horse, Shakespeare would always break his two-day ride at the same tavern in Oxford – then *The Bull*, run by the Davenants, now *The Crown.*
Some people even thought that **William Davenant,** Shakespeare's godson and later a poet and theatre-manager himself, could be Shakespeare's natural son.
→ **Shakespeare's stay at *The Bull* was rather exhausting. You can only manage to walk half the points on your dice with your next throw (odd numbers to be rounded down).**

20 After participating in a rural wedding, Shakespeare sets off with new inspiration:

... ᴀɴᴅ ᴛʜᴇʀᴇ ʀᴇɪɢɴs ʟᴏᴠᴇ ᴀɴᴅ ᴀʟʟ ʟᴏᴠᴇ's ʟᴏᴠɪɴɢ ᴘᴀʀᴛs ...

(Sonnet 31)

→ **You may go three steps further than your dice tells you.**

22 Last overnight stop at **Beaconsfield:**
→ **Miss a turn.**

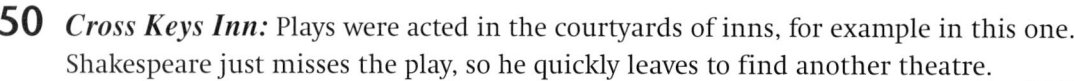

41 Approaching **London** Shakespeare proceeds down what is today the Uxbridge Road through Shepherd's Bush, he goes on via Tyburn, past *Westminster* and *Whitehall* (seat of the government and court) to the city gate near *Blackfriars.*
Blackfriars is a private indoor theatre, the only one licensed by the City authoritities.
But the entrance fee is six times that of the public theatres. The *King's Men* acted here from 1609.
Too expensive for Will, who is now very hungry and tired: all he wants is a pub.
→ **So hurry up and go on twice as far as your dice shows with your next throw to find a pub on the way.**

45 Shakespeare is impressed by **St Paul's.** He listens to the choirboys. They are singers and also actors performing at *Blackfriars.* Shakespeare leaves six coins for the choirboys:
→ **Throw a 6 before moving on.**

50 *Cross Keys Inn:* Plays were acted in the courtyards of inns, for example in this one. Shakespeare just misses the play, so he quickly leaves to find another theatre.
→ **Have two throws of your dice.**

52 There was only one **bridge across the Thames** in Shakespeare's time.
→ **Collect at least 10 points before you can get across the river in the next round. Alternative: The word 'boat' has four letters. Throw a 4 and you can get across by boat with the following throw.**

54 Shakespeare is lucky. There is some *bear-baiting* going on.
ᴛʜᴇʏ ʜᴀᴠᴇ ᴛɪᴇᴅ ᴍᴇ ᴛᴏ ᴀ sᴛᴀᴋᴇ: ɪ ᴄᴀɴɴᴏᴛ ꜰʟʏ,
ʙᴜᴛ, ʙᴇᴀʀʟɪᴋᴇ, ɪ ᴍᴜsᴛ ꜰɪɢʜᴛ ᴛʜᴇ ᴄᴏᴜʀsᴇ. (Macbeth)
➔ **Miss a turn while you watch it.**

57 You must now visit
Shakespeare's theatre: ***The Globe.***
Totus mundus agit histrionem:
This was the *Globe's* motto.
Shakespeare used it in *As You Like It:*
ᴀʟʟ ᴛʜᴇ ᴡᴏʀʟᴅ's ᴀ sᴛᴀɢᴇ
ᴀɴᴅ ᴀʟʟ ᴛʜᴇ ᴍᴇɴ ᴀɴᴅ ᴡᴏᴍᴇɴ ᴍᴇʀᴇʟʏ ᴘʟᴀʏᴇʀs;
➔ **Throw a 2 before you can move on with your next throw.**

60 Shakespeare made a lot of money as actor, playwright and co-owner of the *Globe.*
In Stratford one of the biggest houses in town, ***New Place***, is up for sale and he
wants to hurry back to buy it.
➔ **Collect some money for the journey to Stratford: You need a 6 or a 1 to move on.**

63 Shakespeare spends some time with ***Richard Burbage*** planning
the programme for the time he'll be away.
➔ **Go back to 57: *The Globe.***

67 When he is already on his way, a message from ***the Queen*** reaches
Shakespeare. She wants him to stay and write the second part of his new
play *Henry IV* first. He has to convince the Queen that the play can wait:
➔ **Go back to 42, London.**

69 Shakespeare meets a ***group of players*** on tour. They ask him to stay
the night with them and watch their new play.
➔ **If you throw a 3 or less, you must stay and miss a turn. If you throw a 4 or more,
you thank the players and move on.**

72 At last the silhouette of ***Oxford*** is to be seen in the evening light.
Shakespeare gives his horse the spurs – so he'll soon be at *The Bull.*
After a very late night Shakespeare decides to stay on another day:
➔ **Miss two turns.**

86 Shakespeare has almost reached the city gates of Stratford when he notices
that he left his purse with all his money at ***Banbury*** when buying food from
a *farmer's wife*.
➔ **Go back to Banbury 77 .**

FINISH 90 Shakespeare makes it to Stratford in time. In the spring of 1597 he buys *New Place.*
The house – in a state of some disrepair – only cost him £ 60.
➔ **Congratulations on being back in Stratford. You've made it, but only when you land exactly on 90 !**

   For a different way to play the game, ask your teacher.

Shacosper (4)

This Figure, that thou seest here put,
  It was for gentle Shakespeare cut;
Wherein the Grauer had a strife
  with Nature, to out-doo the life:
O, could he but have drawne his wit
  As well in brasse, as he hath hit
His face, the Print would then surpasse
  All, that was ever writ in brasse.
But, since he cannot. Reader, looke
  Not on his Picture, but his Booke.

From: *The First Folio*

1

Shakeschafte

7

Shaxberd

6

Shaxper

11

Sackesper

Shakestaff

8

3

10

Shackspere

Shakeshafte

Your Shakespeare 🎧

Shagspere

Wm. Shaxpere

Saxber

Shappere

K
Painting by Gerard Soest, **1681**

S
Chandos portrait, possibly painted by Richard Burbage, **late 16th century**

E
From a collection of Shakespeare's works, **19th century**

E
Shakespeare as a man from another planet, **23rd century**

E
Children's painting, **late 20th century**

H
Sculpture near Shakespeare's grave, shortly after **1616**

P
Cover of a book that sees and explains Shakespeare's works in a new light, **1990**

A
Engraving by Droeshout, in the first official book of Shakespeare's works (*First Folio*), published by his friends and colleagues, **1623**

R
Student's sketch, **2001**

A
Advertisement for BBC radio, **1998**

S
Drawing by Picasso, **1964**

- Cut out the pictures and descriptions and make a time line from the first known portrait in Shakespeare's time to the present day. If you get them in the right order, the capital letters on the plates will make sense!

- Which portrait do you think might be closest to what Shakespeare really looked like?

- How did Shakespeare's portrait change during the centuries and what stayed the same?

- Draw your view of William in the empty frame. Add it to your time line.

A Player's Day

Boys began training from the age of ten or so, acting children and pages till they were tall enough to play women. The best might go on till 19, and then become hired men or sharers. Meet Sam, an imaginary player with the Chamberlain's Men, at the theatre, in 1594.

8 am: Sam has been awake since dawn learning a part. 'Run,' yells his master's wife. 'Your master's left. If you're late again, you'll pay the fine, with your pocket money!'

8.15 am: Sam rushes into rehearsal and is grabbed by the bookkeeper. 'Ben's got mumps,' he says. 'You know his lines, don't you? You'll have to take his part as well as yours. They're not on stage together.'

9 am: Rehearsing Shakespeare's play *Two Gentlemen of Verona*. Kempe plays Launce, the comical owner of a dreadful dog. Kempe and the performing dog set the whole cast laughing. Shakespeare begs him not to overdo it.

11.30 am: The play, an old comedy written by Shakespeare, has to be brushed up in a single morning. No time to go out to eat. The boys are sent to get hot pies and order ale for everyone.

12 noon: While munching their pies, the players use the time to consider Shakespeare's new play. He reads it aloud. It sounds promising: good parts, a popular story – *Romeo and Juliet*.

12.15 pm: 'I wrote Juliet's part with Sam in mind,' says Shakespeare. The men roar with laughter, to Sam's great dismay. But they are not laughing at him. The dog has got Shakespeare's pie!

2 pm: *Two Gentlemen* is late starting. Some people in the audience begin to stamp and shout. Sam feels anxious as he is dressed for the sick boy's part. He is not sure that he knows it.

2.30 pm: The boy playing the lady Julia goes on stage and Sam follows as her maid. As he leaves the tiring room he takes a last look at his part to check what he should say.

3.30 pm: All has gone well. The audience is in a good mood now and Sam was word-perfect. In his own part now, the second heroine Silvia, he appears on the gallery, to a serenade.

5.30 pm: Sam hears a row as the money is counted. Old Burbage and Brayne, his partner, keep theirs in a box with two locks. Each partner has a key, and both keys are needed to open the box. 'You're cheating me! You've made a secret key!' yells Brayne.

6.30 pm: Ignoring the quarrel, the cast load up and set off to give a private evening performance. Law students want a play in their dining hall. 'They'll be rowdy after a good dinner,' says Burbage.

10.30 pm: Bed at last. Sam has been given yet another new part to learn. 'I'm too tired now,' he sighs. 'I'll do it in the morning.'

- *What a day! Arrange Sam's activities in the form of a timetable. How much time does he spend on:*
  ❧eating and sleeping? ☼leisure time activities? ☾work in the theatre? ❀work outside the theatre?

- *Make a list of your daily activities.* **What about breakfast? And tea??**

From: Jacqueline Morley and John James: *Shakespeare's Theatre*. Hemel Hempstead, Herts., Simon & Schuster, 1994

The Globe Theatre – An Outdoor Arena

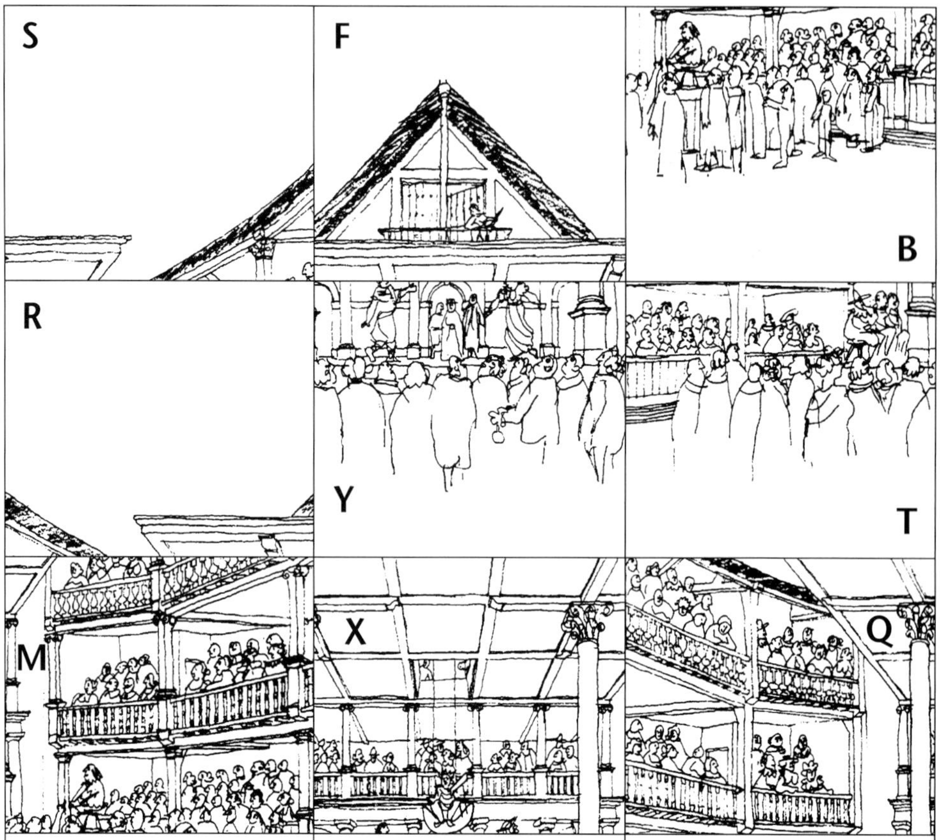

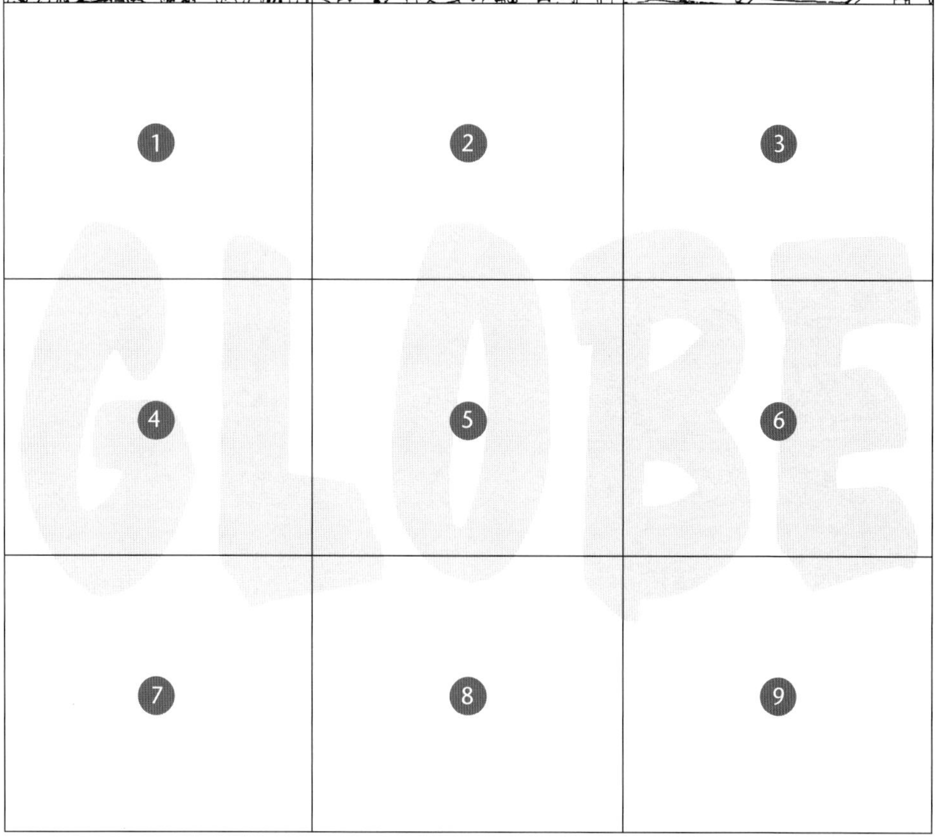

❶ The beginning of a performance was indicated by
T a bell.
X a curtain around the stage being lifted.
R a trumpet.

❷ The most expensive seats were
B right in front of the stage on the ground.
F on or above the stage.
Q opposite the stage on the first balcony.

❸ 'Groundlings' were
S people with cheap tickets standing on the ground around the stage.
M stage workers taking care of the costumes and props in a room under the stage.
X a special kind of rat living in the soft, wet ground near the River Thames.

❹ If a play had night scenes in it,
F it was only put on stage when it was dark enough in the evening.
S a dark curtain helped shadow the stage.
Q various devices, for example a cloth with a moon painted on it, informed the audience about the time of day on stage.

❺ The first English theatre ('The Theatre' in London, 1576) was built
X to have a place that could hold more people than an inn yard or a market place and to make sure they all paid.
R as a present to Queen Elizabeth I.
B to have the actors' apartments and the stage all in one place.

❻ Elizabethan theatres were usually owned by
Y the Queen or by noblemen.
M rich businessmen who rented them to the actors to make money.
T the church in order to prevent indecent plays from being put on stage.

❼ The Burbage brothers, who built the Globe theatre in 1599, were actors and didn't have that much money. So they
B took out a loan from the bank and needed a successful play to earn enough money to pay it back.
T asked other actors to invest money and thus own part of the theatre.
X sold the rights to all the plays of the first five years to Philip Henslowe, another theatre owner.

❽ If gods or angels were in a play, the actors
R jumped from the top balcony, secured by ropes, and swung over the heads of the audience on the ground.
Y were lowered onto the stage from a hidden space above the stage sitting on a wooden bird or cloud.
M explained who they were supposed to be and carried a symbol in their hands.

❾ If a ghost played a role in a play (like in 'Hamlet'),
B it appeared from below the stage through a trapdoor.
S the actor would speak the ghost's lines from behind the stage trying to make his voice sound far away.
Q the actor would hide somewhere on a balcony so the audience wouldn't know where the voice came from.

• *Cut out the pieces of the theatre puzzle.*
• *Read the first question. Decide which one is the right answer, remember the letter that goes with it and find the piece of the puzzle with the same letter. Then glue it in box 1 of the empty grid.*
• *Continue with the following questions until your picture is complete.*

Blackfriars – A Theatre for Rainy Days?

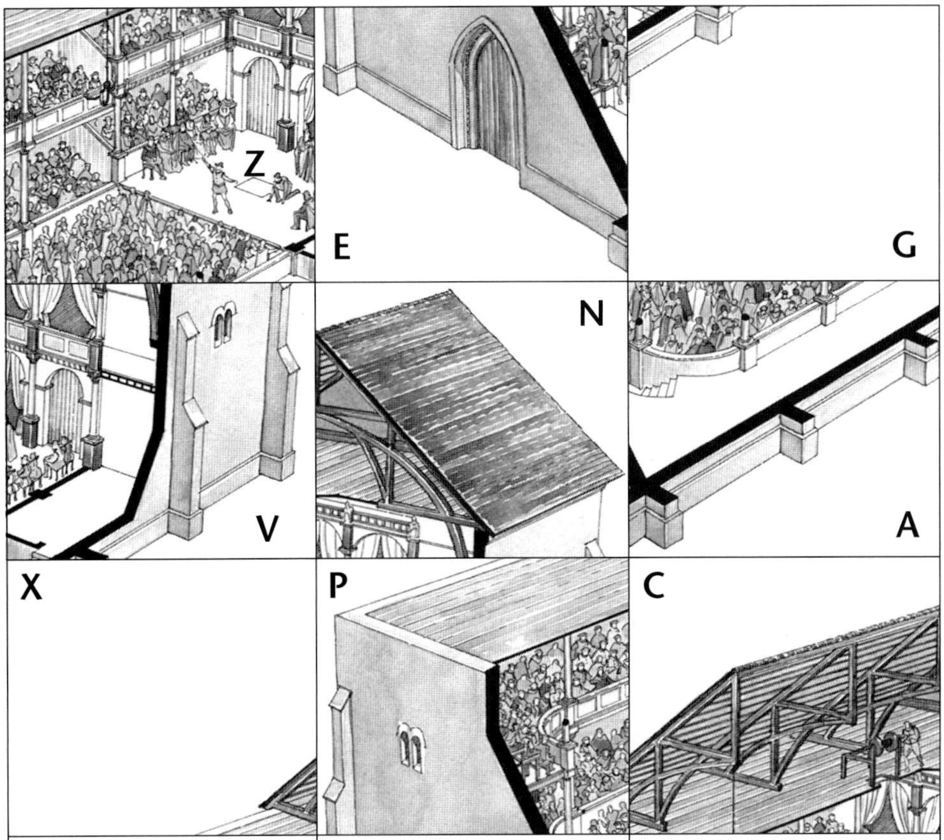

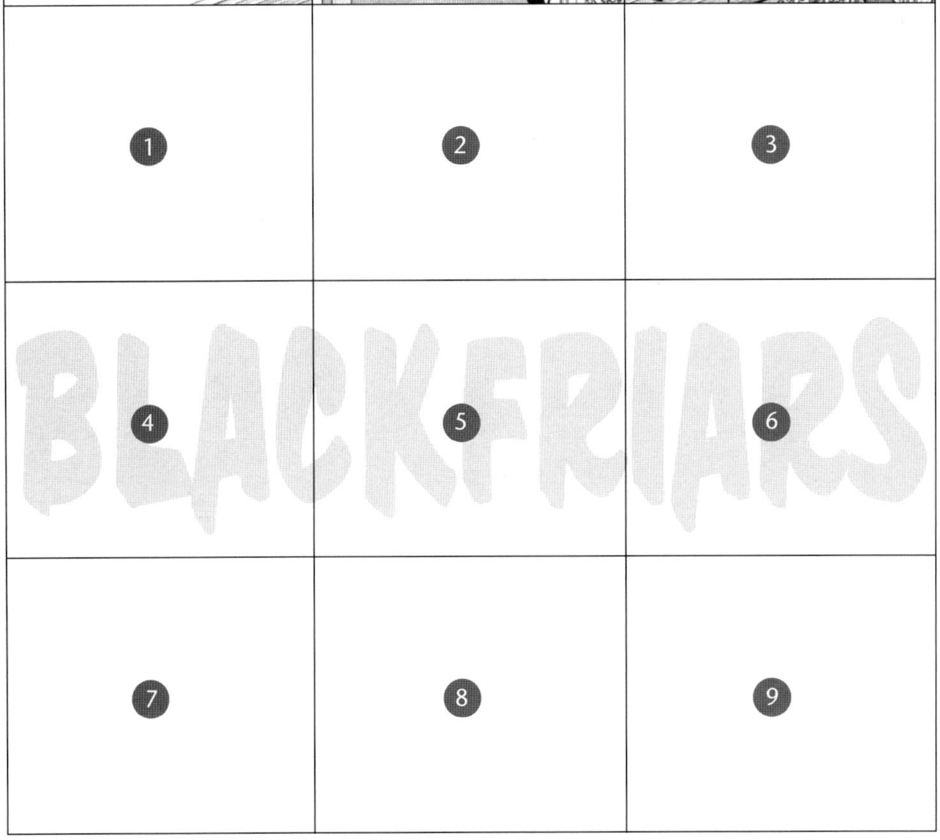

The puzzle grid contains the following labelled pieces:

Z · E · G
N
V · A
X · P · C

1 · 2 · 3

BLACKFRIARS
4 · 5 · 6

7 · 8 · 9

❶ A company of travelling players (for example the King's Men) would choose a nobleman as a patron because
A he paid them.
Z they could then live in his household.
X this showed that they were not homeless people but respectable actors.

❷ A nobleman would give his name to a company of actors because
C their success added to his prestige.
E he received part of the money they earned.
N plays would be written especially for him.

❸ The first indoor theatre, Blackfriars, was (as were all other theatres) closed in 1642 because
G there was a great fire in London and the theatres burnt to the ground.
N the Civil War broke out (Royalists ↔ Parliamentarians).
A there was too much mugging and fighting going on among the audience.

❹ Indoor theatres were six times more expensive than outdoor theatres because
N new plays were first shown there.
P they had fewer seats (only around 800) than outdoor theatres.
V only noblemen were allowed in them.

❺ Intervals were introduced because
X the audience had to be given a chance to go to the toilet.
E the company also organized the sale of food and drink.
Z the theatre was lit by candles which had to be cared for regularly.

❻ Indoor theatres were called 'private' because
E the noblemen wanted to stay among themselves.
V although everybody was allowed in them, they could not be closed down by the city as easily as the public theatres.
Z they belonged to a certain family of nobles.

❼ The Blackfriars Theatre was located in
P an old tavern in which the walls had been blackened by roasting meat on the open fire.
E a closed-down monastery.
X a church building which had never been finished because of financial problems.

❽ The Globe and the Blackfriars both belonged to the 'King's Men', Shakespeare's company of actors. They used Blackfriars
G to put more serious plays on stage.
A mostly in winter time.
C to do private performances for the Queen.

❾ During the first years Burbage, who had built Blackfriars as an indoor theatre, was forced to rent it
G to a group of boy actors who were very popular at the time and took business away from the adult companies.
X to a group of Dominican monks who had lived there before and had returned.
N as a practice room to a sword-fighting school.

- Cut out the pieces of the theatre puzzle.
- Read the first question. Decide which one is the right answer, remember the letter that goes with it and find the piece of the puzzle with the same letter. Then glue it in box 1 of the empty grid.
- Continue with the following questions until your picture is complete.

 # A Day Out in London

I n the summer of 1601 I worked and lived in Master Dale's printing-house in London. Being the youngest apprentice in the shop, there were a lot of rather unpleasant tasks that naturally fell to me: for example scrubbing the ink off the used lead types with a bucket full of piss! Yuk, that stinks so much, especially when it's hot outside.

So I always looked forward to my day off. Living near **St Paul's Cathedral** in the City I used to take the boat down to Bankside whenever I could afford it. But most of the time I had to walk across London Bridge or rather push my way across with crowds of others who were on their way to South Bank.

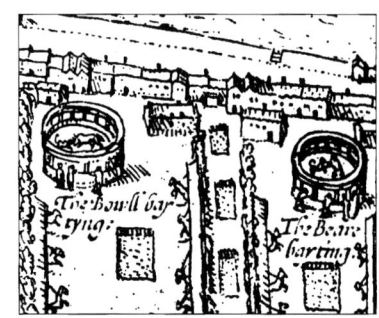

There was a great deal going on in that part of town. There were loads of taverns where you could spend your week's wages on beer. You could go and watch a cockfight or, if you preferred larger animals, have fun at the bull-baiting or **bear-baiting ring**.

I for my part wasn't too keen on seeing blood splatter across the arena. I stuck to the theatres, and my favourite one was the **Globe**. There was blood there too, and fights, tears and screams, but also always something to laugh about. You could go there after lunch, enjoy the performance and be back in the tavern in time to play a game of dice before you went home at night.

On cloudy days I used to go to the tavern directly, as I didn't want to get wet in the theatre in case of a shower. I never wasted money on a gallery seat! For a penny you were allowed to stand on the ground surrounding the stage. That's why this part of the audience was called the *'groundlings'*.

Sitting in the covered galleries was a penny extra, a cushion was another halfpenny. You could even buy stools for sixpence and sit directly on or near the stage. But only rich braggards who wanted to show off their feathered hats and fine clothes wasted their money on things like that. What pests they were! They often interrupted the actors in their speeches, talked among themselves or walked out in the middle of a scene if they didn't like it.

It never got boring in the theatre, believe me! Even if the play was a flop, there was always something to do. The *Globe* could hold nearly 3000 people at a time, and the place wasn't a church. We didn't listen in hushed silence. We talked, bought sausages and fruit from the hawkers who walked round in the playhouse all the time, because there was no break during the performance. And if an apple wasn't good and the play was no better, the apple might very well have landed on the stage or in an actor's face.

Plays changed quickly and there was a great variety offered: comedies, tragedies, histories, romances and sometimes a mixture of them all. Some people liked the slapstick comedies best, others went to see the murders and swordfights, but you always found something you liked.

I personally preferred the magical apparitions, such as ghosts, monsters and witches. They usually jumped out of the middle of nowhere when you least expected it. I loved those scary moments when everybody screamed, beer was tipped over and you held your breath for a moment.

• *Would you rather go and see a performance in an Elizabethan theatre or in a theatre of today?*

Globe-trotting

Many of the greatest plays in the English language were first performed at the original Globe, built in Southwark in 1599. In 1613 the theatre was destroyed by fire when an ember from a stage cannon used in a performance of Henry VIII set light to the thatch.

In 1996, nearly 400 years later, the Globe was reopened only 200 yards from its original site after 40 years of convincing sponsors and raising 30 million pounds of funds.

In the summer before the reconstruction was completely finished actors started exploring the new old stage together with their audience:

■
Shakespeare's
Globe Theatre
Workshop Season

Come to the reconstructed Globe theatre of 1599 in which most of Shakespeare's plays were first performed.

Workshops allow actors and audience to explore afresh the theatre – its acoustics, its atmosphere and the plays.

Be part of a moment in history.
Be part of the Globe Theatre's first audiences for 400 years.
Come and share an adventure.

■Our workshops are not performances – they are dialogues between the director, the actor and the audience. They are demonstrations of the actor's craft. They are the first opportunity to experience what it was like to be in Shakespeare's theatre.

■Each workshop will be introduced by a leading actor or director who will explain the particular theme and lead the audience through an entertaining and often exciting "two hours' traffic of our stage".

■This is the first opportunity for the public to fill the auditorium of the Globe. The promenade area, immediately in front of the stage, is open to the sky and surrounded by three galleries of bench seating under the thatched roof, just as it was in Shakespeare's time.

■Each workshop explores a physical aspect of the Globe. Some deal with how to arrange a battle on the stage – with sword and rapier flying – as fightmasters from America and the UK defend their corner. Other workshops deal with acoustics and techniques for playing on this unusual stage – with the audience clustered around and above the actors.

■Elizabethan actors' physical gestures and use of the stage would seem alien today. Modern theatre commands attention through light and sound. But, in the Globe, actors and audience work together in daylight and players must find ways of focusing the audience's attention without the use of artificial aids.

■There is much to learn ...

- *Make a programme for the workshop season in the Globe. At least three different workshops should be offered.*
- *Prepare these workshops in groups, perhaps using a scene from a Shakespeare play. Recreate the Globe stage and a 'normal' stage with the help of desks and chairs in the classroom. Then do your workshops in class.*

Globe Schools Programme:
http://www.shakespeares-globe.org/education/schools/schools-right.htm

Visiting The 'Rose'

The theatre opens with a new play:

Romeo and Juliet

- Collect information about the theatre building and its various parts such as stage, balconies, ground floor, etc. Look at all the different people you can see: the audience, the actors and others. What do they look like? What are they doing? Where are they sitting? What does the stage look like? How are the actors dressed? What is going on behind the scenes?

- Organize your impressions in a mind map. Don't forget to link your ideas in a well-structured network.
Use different colour pencils for each field of observation.

- Put the mind map on a nice poster so that it becomes a wall display for your classroom. You may add pictures and images which you can get from the Internet, copy from books or any other suitable source.

Why not include some mistakes and see if your classmates can spot them?

Give my friend a beaker of your best brandy. Kit. How goes it, Will? Wonderful. Wonderful. Burbage says you have a play. I have, and the chinks to show for it. I insist, a beaker for Mr Marlowe. I hear you have a new play for 'The Curtain'. Not new, my Dr Faustus. I love your early work: "Is this the face that launched a thousand ships, and burnt the topless towers of Ilium?" I have a new one nearly finished, and better: The Massacre at Paris. Good title. Yours? Romeo and Ethel the Pirate's Daughter. Yes, I know, I know. What is the story? Well, there's this pirate ... in truth I haven't written a word. Romeo, Romeo is Italian, always in and out of love. Yes, that's good. Until he meets ... Ethel. Do you think? The daughter of his enemy. The daughter of his enemy. His best friend is killed in a duel by Ethel's brother, or something. His name is Mercutio. Mercutio, good name. Good luck with yours, Kit. I thought your play was for Burbage. This is a different one. A different one you haven't written?

A Beaker for Mr Marlowe

- With a marker highlight only the parts of the dialogue spoken by Will Shakespeare. Leave Marlowe's text as it is.

- **Pair work:** Discuss with a partner what you will see when you watch the scene.

- **Pair work:** Write down the director's notes for this part of the film. Consider:

- **Group work:** Find another pair of students. Tell them your ideas and make them act out the scene as you would like to have it put on stage.

Follow-up: Compare the life and work of Marlowe and Shakespeare.

Shakespeare in Love 1.27.30

Shakespeare in Love 0.18.00

A Royal Discussion

In this sequence of the film Viola is invited to attend a celebration in the Royal Palace at Greenwich. She meets Queen Elizabeth I, who discusses the merits and benefits of theatre and poetry with her.

Their talk does not get very far because there are so many other people and other matters to attend to.

Viola: Your Majesty.

Elizabeth: Stand up straight, girl. I've seen you. You are the one who comes to all the plays at Whitehall, at Richmond.

Viola: Your Majesty.

Elizabeth: What do you love so much?

Viola: Your Majesty...

Elizabeth: Speak up girl! I know who I am. Do you love stories of kings and queens? Of feats of arms? Or is it courtly love?

Viola: I love theatre. To have stories acted for me by a company of fellows is indeed...

Elizabeth: They're not acted for you, they're acted for me. And?

Viola: And I love poetry above all.

Elizabeth: Above Lord Wessex? My Lord, when you cannot find your wife, you'd better look for her at the playhouse. Playwrights teach us nothing about love. They make it pretty, they make it comical or they make it lust. They cannot make it true.

Viola: Oh, but they can. I mean, your Majesty, they... they do not, they have... not. But I believe there is one who can...

Wessex: My Lady Viola is young in the world. Your Majesty is wise in it. Nature and truth are the very enemies of play acting. I'll wager my fortune on it.

Elizabeth: I thought you were here because you had none. Well, no one will take your wager, it seems.

Nurse: Fifty pounds.

Elizabeth: Fifty pounds? A very worthy sum on a very worthy question. Can a play show us the very truth and nature of love? I bear witness to the wager, and will be the judge of it as occasion arises. I have seen nothing to settle it yet. Are there no more fireworks? They would be soothing after the excitements of Lady Viola's audience. Have her then, but you are a lordly fool. She's been plucked since I saw her last, and not by you. It takes a woman to know it.

Wessex: Marlowe!

- *Read the dialogue and underline the few points that Queen Elizabeth and Viola mention about the merits and benefits of theatre and poetry. Make two lists on the board or on an OHP transparency, one for the Queen, one for Viola. Collect their ideas and put them in the appropriate places.*

- *Watch the video.*

- *Work with a partner. Try to make the dialogue between the Queen and the young lady more substantial by adding more ideas. Partner A collects more ideas for Her Royal Highness, B for Viola.*

> **to wager** *hier:* verwetten
> **to be plucked by somebody**
> somebody else has had her as a lover

- *Collect the ideas of all partners A and B. Use keywords to add them to the lists on the board or the OHP transparency.*

- *Act out the discussion in front of your class by referring to the points mentioned in the lists.*

The Queen's Glove

It is well known that Queen Elizabeth was a great admirer of the immortal Shakspeare, and used frequently (as was the custom with persons of great rank in those days) to appear upon the stage before the audience, or to sit delighted behind the scenes, when the plays of our bard were performed. One evening, when Shakspeare himself was personating the part of a king, the audience knew of Her Majesty being in the house. She crossed the stage when he was performing, and, on receiving the accustomed greeting from the audience, moved politely to the poet, but he did not notice it! When behind the scenes, she caught his eye, and moved again but still he would not throw off his character, to notice her: this made Her Majesty think of some means by which she might know, whether he would depart, or not, from the dignity of his character, while on the stage. – Accordingly, as he was about to make his exit, she stepped before him, dropped her glove, and re-crossed the stage, which Shakspeare noticing, took up, with these words, immediately after finishing his speech, and so aptly were they delivered, that they seemed to belong to it.

> And though now bent on this high embassy,
> Yet stoop we to take up our Cousin's glove!

He then walked off the stage, and presented the glove to the Queen, who was greatly pleased with his behaviour, and complimented him upon the propriety of it.

From: Richard Ryan: *Dramatic Table Talk*, 1825

• *Read the anecdote and then put the pictures in the right order.*

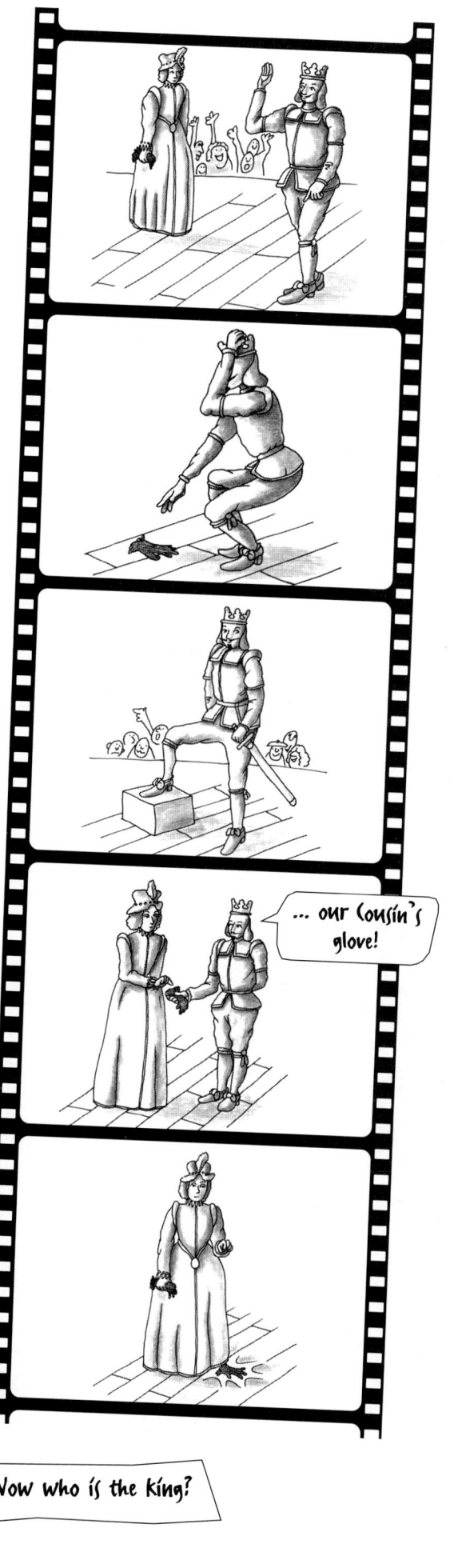

Good Night, Sweet Prince

or what makes some of Shakespeare's plays so boring?

Shakespeare wrote his plays for educated as well as non-educated people, for rich and for poor, because the theatre needed to make money. One or two flops in a row could easily mean unemployment or even the closing down of a theatre. The Globe desperately needed to draw between 1500 and 2000 people per performance and they had to like it so much that they would come back for the next play!

Can you imagine standing in a theatre for four hours without an interval watching a Shakespeare play and still wanting to come back for the next one?
No?
You are in good company.

• Fill in what comes into your mind when you hear the name 'Shakespeare' ...

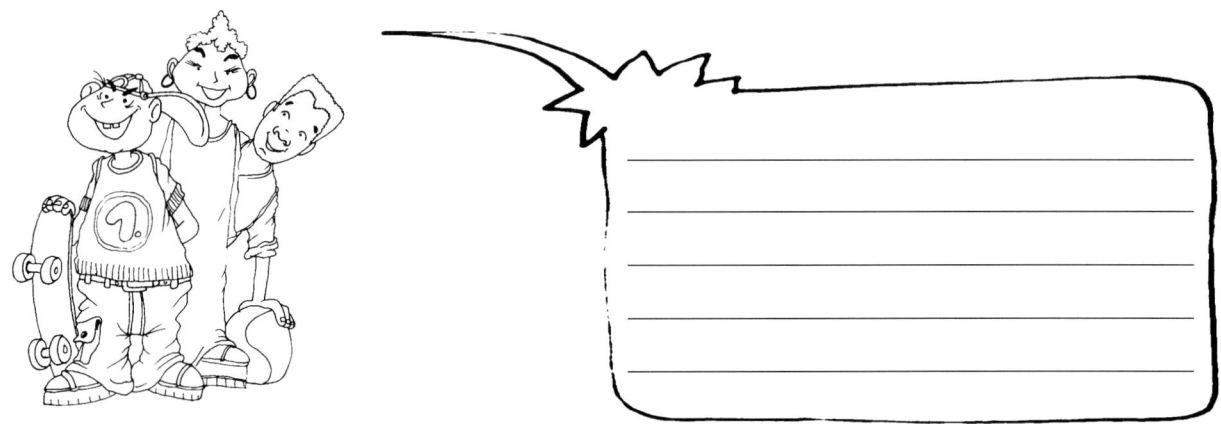

Believe it or not, fun, even in tragedies, was absolutely essential in Shakespeare's day. If the workers hadn't enjoyed themselves after a hard day's or week's work, they wouldn't have spent good money on theatre.

•Arrange a crisis meeting in your class. As directors and players think of ways to pep up a boring theatre performance.

• What makes a theatre performance enjoyable for you?

The actors just had to be very convincing. Otherwise the audience would have thrown apples at them and gone home! By the way, the parts of women were usually played by men.

This is what the Elizabethan writers came up with:

• Find out from the picture what ways Shakespeare used to keep the attention of his audience.

Steal Hamlet ... or else

That's the order from his master. And Widge – a poor orphan with the rare ability to write a unique coded shorthand (which his former master, a rector too busy to write his own Sunday sermons, had taught him) – has no choice but to follow it:

'Now. When you go to London –'

'London?'

'Yes, yes, London. It's a large city to the south of here.'

'I know that, but –'

'Let me finish, then ask questions. When you go to London, you will attend a performance of a play called The Tragedy of Hamlet, Prince of Denmark. You will copy it in Dr Bright's 'shorthand' and you will deliver it to me. Now. Any questions?'

I scarcely knew where to begin. 'I – well, how – that is – they will not object? The men who present the play?'

'Only if they discover you. Naturally you will be as surreptitious as possible.'

'And if they do discover me?' I

> **surreptitious** to do sth. quickly and secretly so nobody notices

asked, thinking of the sermon-copying affair. Bass blew out a cloud of smoke which made me cough.

'The Globe's audience is customarily between five hundred and one thousand. Do you suppose they can watch over every member of it?'

'I wis not.'

'You wis not. Of course they can't. You will use a small tablebook, easily concealed.' He rummaged through the riot of papers on his writing desk. 'You see how easily it is concealed? Even I can't find it.' Finally he came up with a bound pad of paper the size of his hand. 'There. Keep it in your wallet. You have a plumbago pencil?'

'Ay – yes.'

'Any further questions?'

'If I might ask ... for what purpose am I to do this?'

Bass turned a penetrating look on me. 'Does it matter?'

'Nay, I wis not. I was only curious.'

He nodded and scratched the balding top of his head.

'You'll know sooner or later, I suppose.'

He puffed thoughtfully at his pipe, then continued.

> **plumbago** graphite

Shakespeare's *First Folio*

• *Can you imagine why Widge should copy the play?*

Widge's master explains:

'I am a man of business, Widge, and one of my more profitable ventures is a company of players. They are not nearly so successful as the Lord Chamberlain's or the Admiral's Men, but they do a respectable business here in the Midlands. As they have no competent poet of their own, they make do with hand-me-downs [...]. If they could stage a current work, by a poet of some reputation, they could double their box.'

'Box?'

'The money they take in. And my profit would also double. Now someone, sooner or later, will pry [steal] this *Tragedy of Hamlet* from the hands of its poet, Mr Shakespeare, just as they did *Romeo and Juliet* and *Titus Andronicus*.' He jabbed his pipe stem at me for emphasis. 'I would like it to be us, and I would like it to be now, while it is new enough to be a novelty. Besides, if we wait for others to obtain it, they will do a botched [bad] job, patched together from various sources, none of them reliable. Mr Shakespeare deserves better; he is a poet of quality, perhaps of genius, and if his work is to be appropriated [taken away from him], it ought to be done well. That is your mission. If you fulfill it satisfactorily, the rewards will be considerable. If you do not –' He gave a wry [an unpleasant] smile.

'Well, …'

From: Gary Blackwood: *The Shakespeare Stealer.* New York, Dutton, 1998 p. 31 ff.

- *Was your guess (p. 28) right?*
- *Before reading the info box: Imagine you knew shorthand and had to secretly copy a play during a performance. What problems would you expect?*
- *Think of the other people involved in the copying: Widge's master, the theatre company, the author. What does it mean to them?*

INFO Shakespeare never wanted his plays published. He wrote them down as scripts to be used by the actors and he wanted his audience to pay to <u>see</u> the play, not to read it. A good play would surely become a box-office hit and consequently was top secret, so no other company could profit from it. A copyright in the modern sense didn't exist at that time and whoever got hold of the text could use it. So 'word-pirates', like the boy Widge in the story, tried to copy down the play during performances. Naturally, they were full of mistakes …
Seven years after Shakespeare's death two of his friends, the actors Henry Condell and John Heminge, decided to collect their friend's works and publish them in one book called *The First Folio* (1623).
By that time there were so many stolen, bad copies (called bad Quartos) around that they took the risk of publishing the plays.

To be, or not to be, that is the question –
Wether 'tis nobler in the mind to suffer
The slings and arrows of outreageous fortune,
Or to take arms against a sea of troubles,
And, by opposing, end them? To die, to sleep –
No more; and by a sleep to say we end
The heart-ache and the thousand natural shocks
That flesh is heir to. 'Tis a consummation
Devoutly to be wished. To die, to sleep –
To sleep, perchance to dream … ay, there's the rub,
For in that sleep of death what dreams may come,
When we have shuffled off this mortal coil,
Must give us pause. …

The beginning of Hamlet's speech (Act III, Scene 1) in the *First Folio*

To be, or not to be, I there's the point,
To Die, to sleepe, is that all? I all:
No, to sleepe, to dreame, I mary there it goes,
For in that dreamie of death, when wee awake,
And borne before an euerlasting Judge,
From whence no passenger euer retur'nd,
The undiscovered country, at whose sight
The happy smile, and the accursed damn'd.

An example from a bad Hamlet Quarto from 1603

- *Compare the two texts.*
  What is different? What is the same?

Will's Works

```
F O L I O G N I L D N U O R G
T U M T R O I L U S A B N Y T
E W A W I N T E R S N U F O E
L I C Q U S T A L E D R E A M
M W I V E S O F V F C B O N P
A P E K I N G L E A R A M D E
H T H G I N L S N Z E G U S S
O T H E L L O R I W S E C H T
B A R D O F S U C I S V H R W
T P A V O N T O E N I O A E O
W J U L I U S B I D D L D W F
E U F C A E S A R S A B O U T
L L O V E S H L N O T H I N G
F I G H T N A H C R E M L O P
T E R N M I D S U M M E R R Y
H T O D R A H C I R O E M O R
```

There are some titles of Shakespeare's works hidden in this grid.

• *Try and spot them.*

Shakespeare's *First Folio* – the first publication of his works in 1623

The Essential Shakespeare

The Tempest

The First Part of King Henry VI

The Second Part of King Henry VI:

Pericles, Prince of Tyre

Troilus and Cressida

Much Ado About Nothing

As Shakespeare was often in a hurry to get new plays finished in time, he wrote them scene by scene and the players didn't know the end while they were rehearsing the beginning. But with complicated stories the actors were in danger of getting confused. So they pinned short summaries of the scenes to the backstage walls, and in this way they always knew what would happen next.

Titus Andronicus

All's Well That Ends Well

The Two Gentlemen of Verona

A Midsummer Night's Dream

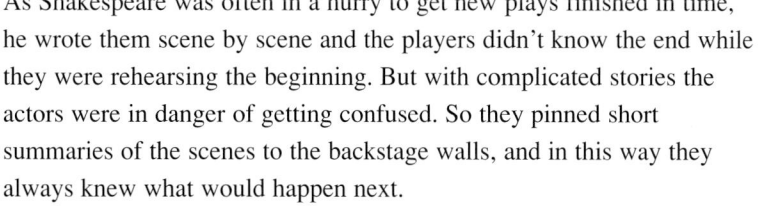

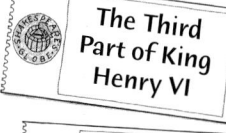The Third Part of King Henry VI

Julius Caesar

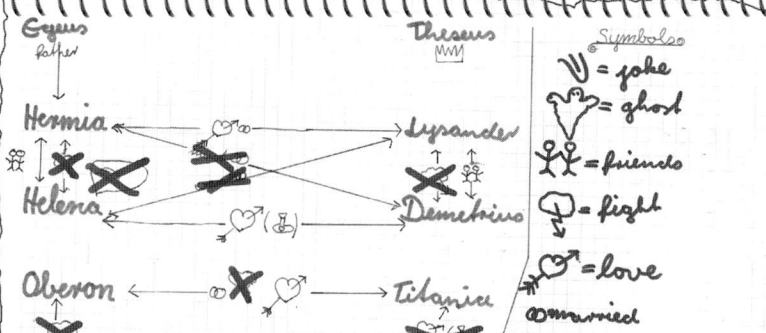

The Merry Wives of Windsor

Measure for Measure

Macbeth

Timon of Athens

The Life of King Henry VIII

The Life and Death of King John

- *Try to retell the story with the help of the 'graphic summary'.*

- *Find out what happens in the play in a dictionary of English literature or any other collection of summaries.*

- *Pick one of Shakespeare's 37 plays. Find out what it is about. Make a 'graphic summary' and sign your name on it. (You can of course use your own symbols.)*

- *Collect all the summaries in class and mix them up:*
  - ➜ *Close your eyes and pick one out at random.*
  - ➜ *Read it through and try to make sense of it.*
  - ➜ *Find the author of your summary.*
  - ➜ *Tell him/her your version of the story.*
  - ➜ *Discuss if and how the summary should be changed to produce the real story.*

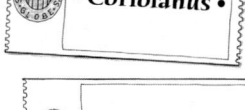Coriolanus

As You Like It

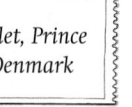

Romeo and Juliet

Cymbeline

The Taming of The Shrew

Hamlet, Prince of Denmark

Love's Labour's Lost

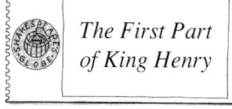The Tragedy of King Richard II

A Midsummer Night's Dream

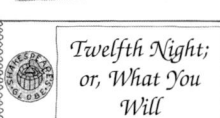Twelfth Night; or, What You Will

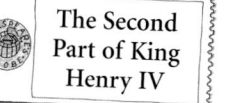The Second Part of King Henry IV

The Tragedy of King Richard III

Othello, The Moor of Venice

The First Part of King Henry

King Lear

The Comedy of Errors

The Merchant of Venice

The Winter's Tale

Antony and Cleopatra

What Joy Is Joy?

An audition is being held at the theatre. Shakespeare is listening to various people who want to be actors.
He is not happy with what he hears. Frustrated, he lies down on a bench, when a young actor called Thomas Kent enters, who recites a soliloquy from *The Two Gentlemen of Verona*.

- *Watch the first sequence depicting the performance of three actors.*

- *They are followed by a young actor who speaks the following lines.*
  Read the soliloquy and practise saying it. Try out various ways of presenting it to an audience.

What light is light, if Silvia be not seen?
What joy is joy, if Silvia be not by?
Unless it be to think that she is by,
And feed upon the shadow of perfection.
Except I be by Silvia in the night,
There is no music in the nightingale;
Unless I look on Silvia in the day,
There is no day for me to look upon.
She is my essence, …

The Two Gentlemen of Verona, Act III, Scene 1

- *Now watch how the actor presents this text to Shakespeare and how he reacts.*
  Compare the different ways the text can be spoken. Choose the one you like best.

- *Write your own love poem by following Shakespeare's pattern.*
  Begin with the question: **What x is x, if y …**
  Then answer it following Shakespeare's pattern:
  Unless …
  Except …

Let Us on Your Imaginary Forces Work ...

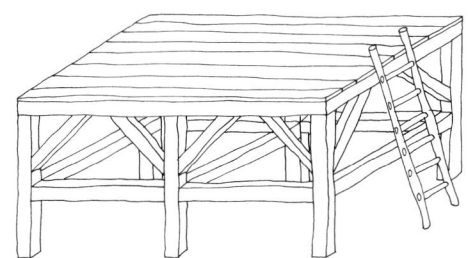

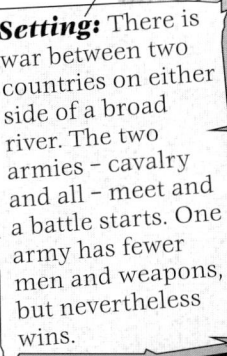

Role card A:
You have been offered a job as a theatre director in a small, very backward town in central Australia. It's an exciting offer, but there are problems:
– You have a very limited budget.
– The stage is outdoors.
– There is no electricity.
But the people in this small town are very enthusiastic about theatre. They are eagerly awaiting you and you are guaranteed a full house for your first performance.

Role card B:
You have been offered a job in Hollywood as the director of an adaptation of Shakespeare's XXX. The producers want you to stage a trial scene.
– Money is no problem.
– You are free to use whatever resources make sense.
Your main aim is to attract people to the cinema.

- Make a plan for staging the above scenes taking into account the information given on your role cards.
- Get together with other students working on the same role card.
  Discuss and compare your suggestions.
- Present the final plan to the group(s) working on the second role card.

Shakespeare was very much in the situation of the Australian outback theatre director. He had to create the scenery, atmosphere and even props using mainly language. So the words spoken on stage had more importance than today: they described what the audience should see in their minds.

➔ Look at the differences in staging the scene. What did you use to make the theatre production attractive, and what did you do to achieve the same effect in the film production?

... Can this cockpit hold
The vasty fields of France? Or may we cram
Within this wooden O the very casques
That did affright the air at Agincourt?
O, pardon: since a crooked figure may
Attest in little place a million;
And let us, ciphers to this great account,
on your imaginary forces work.
Suppose within the girdle of these walls
Are now confined two mighty monarchies,
Whose high upreared and a butting fronts
The perilous narrow ocean parts asunder.
Piece out our imperfections with your thoughts:
Into a thousand parts divide one man,
And make imaginary puissance;
Think, when we talk of horses, that you see them
Printing their proud hoofs i'th'receiving earth;
For 'tis your thoughts that now must deck our kings,
Carry them here and there, jumping o'er times.
...

King Henry V: Chorus, Act I, Scene 1

'Tis now the very witching time of night,
When churchyards yawn, and hell itself
breathes out, Contagion to this world.

Hamlet, Act III, Scene 2

- If you have read or seen other Shakespeare plays: can you find other text passages in which words replace scenery or props?
- Imagine a scene which is very difficult to put on stage (for example, a sunset on the beach ...).

cockpit small space *here:* stage · **vasty** [aː] *(old use)* very large · **to cram** to make fit into a small space **casque** [kæsk] *here:* helmet · **Agincourt** ['ædzɪnkɔːt] famous battle site (1415) in the Hundred Years' War **crooked figure** ['krukɪd] badly written number · **to attest** *here:* to represent · **cipher** ['saɪfə] *here:* sign · **imaginary forces** powers of imagination · **girdle belt** sth. that encircles sth. · **to confine** [-'-] to enclose · **upreared on its back legs** ready to attack · **to abut** to border on **perilous** dangerous · **asunder** apart · **to piece out** *here:* to correct · **puissance** ['pjuːɪsəns] *(old use)* power **to deck** *(old use)* to decorate, to clothe

Henry V – Killer or Hero?

Actor Kenneth Branagh, at age 23 desperately looking for employment, had an interview at the Royal Shakespeare Company (RSC), the theatre company of his dreams:

The real crux of the talk and the offer was Adrian's production of Henry V. [...] He was interested in me but had not [...] seen me in the classics. Perhaps I could go away and prepare a piece of Henry V to come back and work on. I offered to do it there and then.

They took me at my word. Adrian suggested 'Once more unto the breach', and we walked down onto the vast Barbican stage. I put down the book and started. I knew the speech by heart and was so excited that I decided to go for it, regardless. Empty theatres have always thrilled me – the fantastic response with which you can imbue your imaginary audiences can sometimes be more rewarding than the real thing.

Barry and Adrian made helpful comments and I did the speech half a dozen different ways.

'Terrific. We'll be in touch with your agent.'

I suppose that that meant I was through, but I wasn't sure. I didn't dare hope. As I was leaving the stage door, a friend who was in the company rushed up to me.

'Well done, that was great.'

'What was?'

'Your audition.'

'How do you know?'

'The tannoy and the video monitor were both on. We were all in the green room having a bite between shows and cheering you on.'

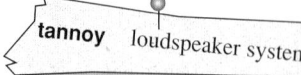
tannoy   loudspeaker system

'Bloody 'ell.'

'I'm sure you've got it.'

He was right. [...]

Two years employment. [...] Henry V opened the Stratford season, and if it was a disaster, I'd either be kicked out or have to suffer it for two years.

From: Kenneth Branagh: *Beginning*, London: Pan Books, 1989, p. 134 f.

Henry V is in France and attacks the city of Harfleur.

To raise his soldiers' aggressiveness Henry gives a fiery speech:

Once more unto the breach, dear friends, once more,
Or close the wall up with our English dead.
In peace there's nothing so becomes a man
As modest stillness and humility:
But when the blast of war blows in our ears,
Then imitate the action of the tiger;
Stiffen the sinews, conjure up the blood,
Disguise fair nature with hard-favour'd rage;
Then lend the eye a terrible aspect;
Let it pry through the portage of the head
Like the brass cannon; let the brow o'erwhelm it
As fearfully as doth a galled rock
O'erhang and jutty his confounded base,
Swill'd with the wild and wasteful ocean.
Now set the teeth and stretch the nostril wide,
Hold hard the breath, and bend up every spirit
To his full height! On, on, you noblest English!
Whose blood is fet from fathers of war-proof;

Fathers that, like so many Alexanders,
Have in these parts from morn till even fought,
And sheath'd their swords for lack of argument.
Dishonour not your mothers; now attest
That those whom you call'd fathers did beget you.
Be copy now to men of grosser blood,
And teach them how to war. And you, good yeomen,
Whose limbs were made in England, show us here
The mettle of your pasture; let us swear
That you - are worth your breeding; which I doubt not;
For there is none of you so mean and base
That hath not noble lustre in your eyes.
I see you stand like greyhounds in the slips,
Straining upon the start. The game's afoot:
Follow your spirit; and upon this charge
Cry, 'God for Harry, England, and Saint George!'

From: King Henry V, Act III, Scene 1

- *Get together in groups of five and read Henry's speech. Then each of you takes one of the following roles:*
  - *Kenneth Branagh (young actor, looking for employment)*
  - *Barry Kyle (senior director at the RSC)*
  - *Adrian Noble (director of Henry V at the RSC)*
  - *Two young colleagues having a snack in the cafeteria and watching the audition on the video screen*

- *'Branagh' gives his speech (in parts) and directors and colleagues give advice and comment until you have the final version with which everyone is satisfied.*

- *Discuss in class what you felt when you played your role:*
  Was it easy/difficult to identify with the text? What image of Henry did you have in mind when speaking/directing/commenting on the scene ... ?

Henry V invaded France but talked of sin, conscience and guiltless blood being shed in his wars.
In the Second World War the play was enormously popular in England, today people often have an uneasy feeling
about it, just like actor Kenneth Branagh when he was rehearsing the part:

The major problems by the eighth week [...] were two elusive areas of Henry's experience. The first was war, and I tried to do something about this by reading Clausewitz, Sassoon, historical documents about the combat detail at Agincourt. I was very slowly beginning to picture the horrors of a hand-to-hand medieval combat. It was quite easy to get a graphic impression of what fighting could be like from people in the company. Sebastian Shaw, for instance, had been in the RAF during the Second World War, and his account of the terror of a 'night raid' was a chilling highlight of one of several fascinating rehearsal discussions. But it was much more difficult to get my imagination around Henry's royal status, the isolation of his role as spiritual and military leader. Quite simply, what was it like being a king? As with war there was plenty of written material, but there was no one to talk to, no one with whom I could exchange ideas. [...]

Through friends the young actor gets an invitation to meet Prince Charles.

A week later I was motoring up the long gravel drive to Kensington Palace. [...]My grubby green car came to a halt by the security hut, and the policeman waved me through. My God, they really did expect me. I walked to the front door without being ambushed by three hundred security guards and when the door opened the footman greeted me with, 'Mr Branagh?'
I waited downstairs in a room filled with Royal Wedding memorabilia. [...] I wondered with alarm what exactly I was going to ask the heir to the throne, but the time for panicking was over, and I was shown upstairs and into the Prince's drawing-room where he shook my hand warmly, smiled and said, 'I really have no idea how I can help you, but please sit down, and let's have a chat.' [...]
'Well, sir, I know it seems rather strange. I'm not intending my Henry V to be an impersonation of you, but I simply wanted to explain some of my feelings about the character, particularly his role as king. They're not necessarily highly academic or intellectual observations, but as you're in a unique position to comment, I'd love to run them past you, and if you have anything to say about them I'd be most grateful.'

[...] by the time I had left I was aware of having met a very remarkable man. He did not possess the same power as Henry, but his influence was considerable [...]

I had no desire to beg an audience's forgiveness for a man who had invaded another country on dubious pretexts and with enormous loss of life. They had to make up their own minds about the fascinating, enraging conflict between the ruthless killer and the Christian king.

From: Kenneth Branagh: *Beginning*, London, Pan Books, 1989, p. 141 ff.

Is it true that being a king involves suppressing many facets of one's character? You can't really be who you are and the suppressed parts of your character will come up from time to time with tremendous force. Henry, for example, seems to suppress his sense of humour and his latent violence.

Henry is very isolated and feels lonely and rather melancholic. Is it a problem for you when press and media invade your privacy and you just can't move around like other men?

I feel that as Henry couldn't really turn to anyone for help, his only real comfort was faith. Does being religious help a king?

- *How do you think Prince Charles answered? Act out an interview with Charles.*

- *Find evidence in the play for each of Branagh's assumptions about Henry V's role as king.*
  *Some hints where to look: Act IV, Scene 1: '**Upon the king!**'; Act 1, Scene. 1, etc.*

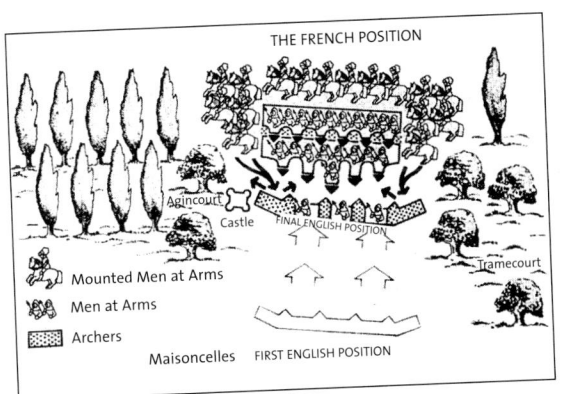

THE FRENCH POSITION

Agincourt Castle

FINAL ENGLISH POSITION

Tramecourt

Mounted Men at Arms

Men at Arms

Archers

Maisoncelles   FIRST ENGLISH POSITION

Agincourt

In 1340 Edward III proclaimed himself 'King of England and France' and so instituted a claim which the English struggled for over 100 years to maintain. The battle of Agincourt was a blow in that struggle.

When Henry V came to the throne in 1413, France had been in a state of civil war for six years. Old King Charles VI suffered from intermittent madness, his brother the Duke of Orleans had been murdered by John the Fearless, Duke of Burgundy, and the body of the country was split apart by the struggling factions. With the realm divided against itself, it was an ideal time for Henry to invade.

When he set off to Southampton for what he planned to be a ten-week campaign (though in fact it ran into fifteen weeks), he had 10,000 men, many of whom were volunteers.

Their enthusiasm must have taken an early blow – with 25,000 horses to load onto the ships (none of which was more than 500 tons) embarkation took two weeks, and once on board, the soldiers had to spend a further 18 cramped, swaying days in their quarters waiting for a wind to France.

They finally arrived at what is now Le Havre and marched to besiege the town of Harfleur, which fell to them with little struggle.

Despite their easy victory, the state of the army was already poor. In some ways the archers weren't too badly off. Each had embarked with a quiver of about thirty arrows, and after a battle he was quite often able to retrieve those he had shot and, if they needed repair, send them off to the travelling armourers. But the weather was wet and the going marshy – iron weapons and armour were rusting and the men's light felt and leather boots were disintegrating faster than the cobblers could mend them. Besides there was dysentery. More men fell by the way from that than from the wounds of battle. They were down to 7,000 men and the supplies of bread and the hated salt-pork were running low. Henry decided to return to England to recuperate. The march towards Calais was punishing: they covered 250 miles in 20 days. But before they reached the coast they found the French in their path.

From: RSC-programme: *Henry V*, 1976

quiver a case for carrying arrows

dysentery an infection that makes you go to the toilet constantly

Hamlet: A Ghostly Interview

ACT I, SCENE 1

HORATIO

1   Well sit we down,
     And let us hear Bernardo speak of this.

BERNARDO

     Last night of all,
     When yond same star that's westward from the

5   pole
     Had made his course t'illume that part of heaven
     Where now it burns, Marcellus and myself,
     The bell then beating one -
          Enter Ghost.

Bernardo describes _____

_____

MARCELLUS

10   Peace, break thee off. Look where it comes again.

BERNARDO

     In the same figure, like the king that's dead.

MARCELLUS

     Thou art a scholar; speak to it, Horatio.

BERNARDO

     Looks 'a not like the king? Mark it, Horatio.

HORATIO

     Most like. It harrows me with fear and wonder.

BERNARDO

15   It would be spoke to.

Horatio should speak to the ghost because _____

_____

MARCELLUS

     Question it, Horatio.

HORATIO

     What art thou that usurp'st this time of night
     Together with that fair and warlike form
     In which the majesty of buried Denmark

20   Did sometimes march? By heaven I charge thee,
     speak!

MARCELLUS

     It is offended.

BERNARDO

     See, it stalks away.

HORATIO

     Stay! Speak, speak! I charge thee, speak!
          Exist Ghost.

Horatio wants to know _____

_____

He wants the ghost to _____

but the ghost _____

MARCELLUS

25   'Tis gone and will not answer.

BERNARDO

     How now, Horatio? You tremble and look pale.
     Is not this something more than fantasy?
     What think you on't?

ACT I, SCENE 4

Enter Hamlet, Horatio, and Marcellus.

HAMLET

The air bites shrewdly; it is very cold.

HORATIO

It is a nipping and an eager air.

HAMLET

What hour now?

HORATIO

I think it lacks of twelve.

MARCELLUS

5 No, it is struck.

HORATIO

Indeed? I heard it not. It then draws near the season
Wherein the spirit held his wont to walk.
[…]

Enter Ghost.

HORATIO   Look, my lord, it comes.

HAMLET

Angels and ministers of grace defend us!
10 Be thou a spirit of health or goblin damned,
Bring with thee airs from heaven or blasts from
hell,
Be thy intents wicked or charitable,
Thou com'st in such a questionable shape
15 That I will speak to thee. I'll call thee Hamlet,
King, father, royal Dane. O, answer me!
[…]

HORATIO

It beckons you to go away with it,
As if in some impartment did desire
To you alone.

MARCELLUS

20 Look with what courteous action
It waves you to a more removed ground.
But do not go with it.

HORATIO   No, by no means.

HAMLET

It will not speak. Then
25 I will follow it.

HORATIO   Do not, my lord.

HAMLET

Why, what should be the
fear?
I do not set my life at a
pin's fee,
30 And for my soul, what can it do
to that,
Being a thing immortal as itself?
It waves me forth again; I'll follow it.

Weather: _____

Time: _____

What should happen at that time _____
_____

Hamlet wonders whether the ghost _____
_____

The ghost wants Hamlet to come with him because
_____
_____
_____

Hamlet is not
afraid because

_____

_____

_____

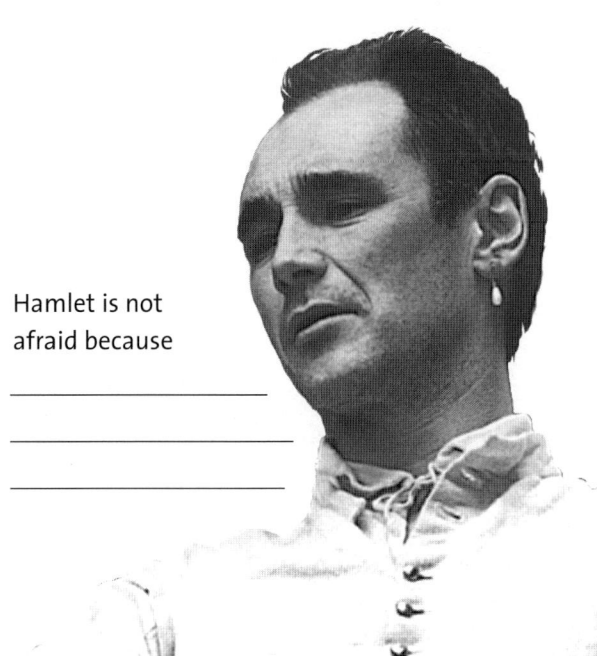

ACT I, SCENE 5

Enter Ghost and Hamlet.

HAMLET
    Whither wilt thou lead me? Speak. I'll go no further.

GHOST   **Mark me.**

HAMLET   **I will.**

GHOST
    My hour is almost come,

5   **When I to sulph'rous and tormenting flames**
    Must render up myself.

HAMLET   **Alas, poor ghost!**

GHOST
    Pity me not, but lend thy serious hearing
    To what I shall unfold.

10 HAMLET   **Speak. I am bound to hear.**

GHOST
    So art thou to revenge, when thou shalt hear.

HAMLET   **What?**

GHOST   **I am thy father's spirit,**
    Doomed for a certain term to walk the night,

15   **And for the day confined to fast in fires,**
    Till the foul crimes done in my days of nature
    Are burnt and purged away. But that I am forbid
    To tell the secrets of my prison-house,
    I could a tale unfold whose lightest word

20   **Would harrow up thy soul, freeze thy young blood,**
    Make thy two eyes like stars start from their
    spheres,
    Thy knotted and combinèd locks to part,
    And each particular hair to stand on end

25   **Like quills upon the fretful porpentine.**
    But this eternal blazon must not be
    To ears of flesh and blood. List, list, o, list!
    If thou didst ever thy dear father love –

HAMLET   **O God!**

30 GHOST   **Revenge his foul and most unnatural murder.**

HAMLET   **Murder!**

GHOST   **Murder most foul, as in the best it is;**
    But this most foul, strange, and unnatural.

Hamlet wants to know _____

The ghost asks Hamlet to _____

Very soon the ghost will have to _____

The ghost wants Hamlet to _____
and then to _____

The ghost must not _____
_____

What would happen if he did? _____
_____

The ghost's story: . . . .

- *After listening to the scenes, read them slowly on your own. Then discuss sections you don't understand with a partner and try to fill in the answers together. Most difficult parts can be guessed from the context or from thinking logically.*

- *Get together in groups of five (four actors, one director) and rehearse one of the scenes. When you feel ready, present it to the class.*

Bitten by a Snake?

The king of Denmark was found dead in his garden, bitten by a snake, the official report said. But how many poisonous snakes are there in Denmark, in a royal garden? Anyway, some people started to suspect that something was wrong, very wrong. But nobody dared say anything when the king's brother, Claudius, married Gertrude, the king's widow, and soon afterwards claimed the throne and did everything he could to make people forget what had happened. Although the old king had been very popular and Claudius didn't compare to him at all, the ladies and gentlemen of the court tried to please the new king. They danced at his balls, tried to look as if they were having a lot of fun at court.

All but one – Prince Hamlet! As if to provoke people, he constantly wore black mourning clothes, never laughed and kept dropping gloomy hints about his father's death. He became more and more depressed, and the world seemed so empty and absurd to him that he even wished he were dead too! 'What a life!' he thought. 'My father dead, a stupid king on the throne, and if my mother had loved her husband she wouldn't have married again so soon! If only I knew more about his death!'

Some days later Horatio, a friend of Hamlet's, told him about a strange thing that had happened on the battlements of the fortress of Elsinore, where the king lived: A ghost in the shape of Hamlet's father had appeared at night but had spoken to nobody. Hamlet decided to find out what was going on there. He waited for the ghost to come again and – it did! The ghost made Hamlet follow him until they were alone and then he told the frightened prince all about his death: Yes, he had been murdered, and in a sneaky and cowardly way, too. He had been murdered by ?????

Here are the suspects:

Ophelia,
Polonius's daughter,
in love with Hamlet

King Claudius,
the murdered King's brother

Queen Gertrude,
the murdered King's wife
and now Claudius's wife

Polonius and his son Laertes,
both noblemen who work for the King;
both think Hamlet is not serious about Ophelia.

- *Who had reason enough to kill the King?*
  Think about the suspects' motives. Who really benefits from the murder? Who could have benefited? Also think about who actually should have succeeded the old King. Check for clues in the text first, then use your imagination.

☠ Murder Most Foul, Strange and Unnatural ☠

I

Murder? Yes, it was murder. His own brother had poured poison into old King Hamlet's ear while he was sleeping in the garden. The ghost told Prince Hamlet all about it and finally made him swear that he wouldn't let Claudius go on like this. Revenge had to be taken, and who could do that better than the victim's own son, young Hamlet?

> **I. GHOST: IF THOU HAST NATURE IN THEE, BEAR IT NOT.**

II

After he had sworn to do something about the situation, Hamlet just couldn't decide how to go about it. He was shocked and frightened, and he feared the King and Queen might suspect that he knew how his father had died. This seemed especially likely since they were already watching him carefully. So the Prince decided to act stranger than ever. He didn't care about his clothes any more, said things nobody could understand and, in short, behaved like a real madman.

> **II. HAMLET** (*mad*): **I AM BUT MAD NORTH-NORTH-WEST: WHEN THE WIND IS SOUTHERLY, I KNOW A HAWK FROM A HANDSAW.**

III

'What in the world happened to young Hamlet?', everybody wondered until one day it became known that the Prince was in love with pretty Ophelia, the daughter of Polonius, who was a counsellor to the King. Since Polonius was not sure whether Hamlet was just looking for a romantic adventure with Ophelia, after which he would leave her, he forbade her to be friendly with Hamlet. Why should not his love have made him mad? Yes, that was the solution!

> **III. POLONIUS** (*zu Ophelia*): **LORD HAMLET IS A PRINCE OUT OF THY STAR, THIS MUST NOT BE.**

IV

But Claudius wanted to be sure that Hamlet couldn't do him any harm. So he planned to send him away to England and have him murdered on the way just to be on the safe side, in case he knew more after all! Hamlet knew about his uncle's plans and still he didn't do anything. He was continually worried by the memory of the ghost. What if the apparition hadn't spoken the truth?

> **IV. CLAUDIUS: MADNESS IN GREAT ONES MUST NOT UNWATCHED GO.**

V

One evening, as a group of actors was getting ready to perform in the castle, Hamlet suddenly had an idea. He knew a play that was about the murder of a king by his own brother: The Murder of Gonzago. He changed the play a little bit so that it resembled very much the real murder of his father. He planned to watch Claudius's face when he saw his own crime on the stage. The play began and the King and Queen seemed to be in the best of moods. But as the play progressed they grew more and more anxious, and all of a sudden Claudius jumped to his feet and ran out of the room. Now there couldn't be any doubt: he, and nobody else, had murdered King Hamlet!

> **V. HAMLET: I'LL HAVE THESE PLAYERS PLAY SOMETHING LIKE THE MURDER OF MY FATHER BEFORE MINE UNCLE; I'LL OBSERVE HIS LOOKS.**

VI

While the Prince was still thinking about what to do now, his mother sent for him. She hoped to be able to find out what all these strange actions meant, and she asked Polonius to hide in her room so he could hear everything Hamlet said. On his way to his mother's room Hamlet by chance saw Claudius kneeling on the floor and praying to God. He couldn't see Hamlet approach. Should he do it now? It would be so easy! Just draw the sword … But then Claudius would go straight to heaven, since he had been killed while praying. No, he didn't deserve that.

> **VI. CLAUDIUS** *(praying)*: **MY WORDS FLY UP, MY THOUGHTS REMAIN BELOW. WORDS WITHOUT THOUGHTS NEVER TO HEAVEN GO.**

VII

Hamlet was angry with his mother. He screamed at her and told her all kinds of unpleasant things until she got so frightened that she cried out for help. Something behind a curtain moved, Hamlet drew his sword – one thrust and Polonius, who had been standing there listening, fell to the ground, dead.

To kill a nobleman without sufficient reason was a serious crime, and so Claudius finally had an excuse to send Hamlet away to England and carry out his plan for murdering him.

> **VII. CLAUDIUS: NOW, HAMLET, WHERE IS POLONIUS?**
> **HAMLET: AT SUPPER.**
> **CLAUDIUS: AT SUPPER! WHERE?**
> **HAMLET: NOT WHERE HE EATS, BUT WHERE 'A IS EATEN.**

VIII

Hamlet, of course, didn't trust his uncle. He made him think that he was going abroad, but came back secretly at night. On his way back to Elsinore he had to pass a graveyard and, late as it was, there seemed to be a funeral taking place. He stopped to watch: The King , the Queen and other nobles were there and, in a coffin, Ophelia! Wild with grief, Hamlet found out that she had gone mad when she had heard that her lover had killed her father. In her madness she had fallen into the river and died, or had she jumped?

> **VIII. GERTRUDE** *(throwing flowers in the grave)*: **SWEETS TO THE SWEET: FAREWELL.**

IX

But Hamlet wasn't the only one who was sad about Ophelia's death. Her brother Laertes was also sad and at the same time angry with Hamlet. Hamlet had caused all the problems, had killed his father and sister. Claudius suddenly saw another way of getting rid of Hamlet without killing him himself. Why shouldn't Laertes fight against the Prince and revenge his family? To make sure Hamlet wouldn't survive this duel in any case, Claudius gave Laertes a very sharp sword with a poisoned tip and also prepared a cup of poisoned wine. If Hamlet won the fight, he could drink with him and he would make sure Hamlet got the right cup.

> **IX. CLAUDIUS** *(zu Laertes)*: **REVENGE SHOULD HAVE NO BOUNDS.**

X

The next day the King, the Queen and all the nobles gathered to watch the fight. Laertes was very good at swordfighting, so Claudius watched quite calmly, but then – Hamlet wasn't bad either … the duel went on and on with everybody watching breathlessly. Then suddenly Laertes cut Hamlet slightly on his hand, whereupon Hamlet seized his enemy's sword and cut Laertes with his own weapon … Meanwhile Gertrude had picked up a cup of wine that had been standing near her – it was the poisoned cup! In a minute she fell down – dead. Laertes then told Hamlet all about the King's intrigues and begged the Prince to forgive him. They both had only a few more minutes to live. And Claudius? Is his plan still going to work out? His greatest enemy is dying right in front of his eyes. Hamlet grabs the poisoned sword and runs towards the King.

> **X. HORATIO: GOOD NIGHT, SWEET PRINCE, AND FLIGHTS OF ANGELS SING THEE TO THY REST!**

Then venom, do thy work!

The rest is? E L S I N C

Pantomimic presentation of Hamlet in ten parts

- *Together with one or two partners pick a scene of the story you like. Talk about how it could best be presented 'silently', i.e. without text, just with the help of mime, props, etc. Make a short written plan for the presentation of your scene, so you'll have something to refer to.*

To Do it or not to Do it

In the very first act the ghost tells Hamlet exactly what to do, but it takes over four hours playing time until Hamlet finally does what the ghost asked him to do:

The ghost told Hamlet to murder Claudius.

In the course of the play seven people get killed.

- *Fill in the flow chart with the steps that lead to the final action and note down the names of all the people that die on the way.*

- *Can you imagine why it took Hamlet so long to do what the ghost had told him? Find at least five possible reasons, discuss them in class and then rank them on a scale between 1 and 5, 1 being the most important reason, 5 the least important one.*

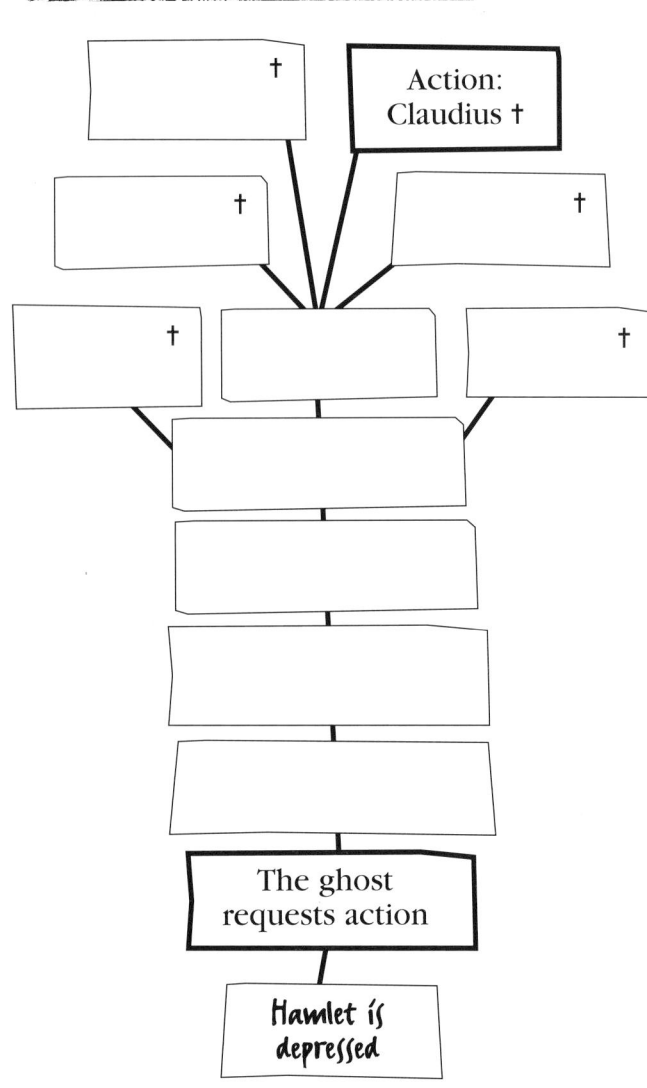

Action:
Claudius †

The ghost
requests action

Hamlet is
depressed

Shakespeare – Dead Boring?

This is an extract from Willy Russell's play *Educating Rita* (1981). Rita is a hairdresser who attends a summer course about literature at the Open University. Frank is her professor. After seeing Shakespeare's play *Macbeth* in the theatre, she rushes into Frank's study to tell him about the impact the play had on her:

Rita   I had to come an'tell y', Frank, last night, I went to the theatre! A proper one, a professional theatre.
Frank gets up and switches off the radio and then returns to the swivel chair.

Frank   *(sighing)* For God's sake, you had me worried, I thought it was something serious.

Rita   No, listen, it was. I went out an' got me ticket, it was Shakespeare. I thought it was gonna be dead borin'...

Frank   Then why did you go in the first place?

Rita   I wanted to find out. But listen, it wasn't borin', it was bleedin' great, honest, ogh, it done me in, it was fantastic. I'm gonna do an essay on it.

> **it done me in**
> I was overwhelmed by it

Frank   *(smiling)* Come on, which one was it?
Rita moves URC.

> **URC**   upstage right centre

Rita   '... Out, out, brief candle!
Life's but a walking shadow, a poor player
That struts and frets his hour upon the stage
And then is heard no more. It is a tale

Told by an idiot, full of sound and fury
Signifying nothing.'

Frank   *(deliberately)* Ah, Romeo and Juliet.

Rita   *(moving towards Frank)* Tch. Frank! Be serious. I learnt that today from the book. *(She produces a copy of* Macbeth*)* Look, I went out an' bought the book. Isn't it great? What I couldn't get over is how excitin' it was.
Frank puts his feet up on the desk.
Wasn't his wife a cow, eh? An' that fantastic bit where he meets Macduff an' he thinks he's all invincible. I was on the edge of me seat at that bit. I wanted to shout out an' tell Macbeth, warn him.

Frank   You didn't, did you?

Rita   Nah. Y' can't do that in a theatre, can y'? It was dead good. It was like a thriller.

Frank   Yes. You'll have to go and see more.

Rita   I'm goin' to. (...)

From: Willy Russell: *Educating Rita*. Frankfurt am Main, Berlin, München: Diesterweg 1984, pp. 45 f.

- *Why did Rita go to the theatre, do you think?*

> **Why did Rita not warn Macbeth??**

> **Why does she want to write an essay?**

- *Write the essay from Rita's point of view.*

Macbeth's a Tragedy, isn't it?

Rita   [...] *Macbeth*'s a tragedy, isn't it?
Frank nods
Right.
Rita smiles at Frank and he smiles back at her. Well I just – I just had to tell someone who'd understand.

Frank   I'm honoured that you chose me.

Rita   *(moving towards the door)* Well, I better get back. I've left a customer with a perm lotion. If I don't get a move on there'll be another tragedy.

Frank   No. There won't be a tragedy.

Rita   There will, y' know. I know this woman; she's dead fussy. If her perm doesn't come out right there'll be blood an' guts everywhere.

Frank   Which might be quite tragic – *(he throws her the apple from his desk, which she catches)* – but it won't be a tragedy.

Rita   What?

Frank   Well – erm – look; the tragedy of the drama has nothing to do with the sort of tragic event you're talking about. Macbeth is flawed by his ambition – yes?

Rita   *(going and sitting in the chair by the desk)* Yeh. Go on. *She starts to eat the apple*

Frank   Erm – it's that flaw which forces him to take the inevitable steps towards his own doom. You see? *Rita offers him the can of soft drink. He takes it and looks at it.*
(putting the can down on the desk) No thanks. Whereas, Rita, a woman's hair being reduced to an inch of stubble, or – or the sort of thing you read in the paper that's reported as being tragic, 'Man Killed By Falling tree' is not a tragedy.

Rita   It is for the poor sod under the tree.

Frank   Yes, it's tragic, absolutely tragic. But it's not a tragedy in the way that Macbeth is a tragedy. Tragedy in dramatic terms is inevitable, preordained. Look, now, even without ever having heard the story of Macbeth you wanted to shout out, to warn him and prevent him going on, didn't you? But you wouldn't have been able to stop him, would you?

Rita   No.

Frank   Why?

Rita   They would have thrown me out the theatre.

Frank   But what I mean is that your warning would have been ignored. He's warned in the play. But he can't go back. He still treads the path to doom. But the poor old fellow under the tree hasn't arrived there by following any inevitable steps, has he?

Rita   No.

Frank   There's no particular flaw in his character that has dictated his end. If he'd been warned of the consequences of standing beneath that particular tree he wouldn't have done it, would he? Understand?

Rita   So – so Macbeth brings it on himself?

Frank   Yes. You see, he goes blindly on and on and with every step he's spinning one more piece of thread which will eventually make up the network of his own tragedy. Do you see?

Rita   I think so. I'm not used to thinkin' like this.

Frank   It' quite easy, Rita.

Rita   It is for you. I just thought it was a dead excitin' story. But the way you tell it you make me see all sorts of things in it. *(after a pause)* It's fun, tragedy, isn't it? [...]

From: Willy Russell: *Educating Rita*. Frankfurt am Main. Berlin. München: Diesterweg 1984, pp. 46f.

- *Continue the dialogue.*
- *Act it out and possibly film it.*
- *Rita and Frank have different views of 'tragedy' and 'tragic': What do you think?*

Is this a Dagger ...

In the film *Dead Poets Society* Keating, a teacher of English literature, is talking about Shakespeare.

He imitates various ways of reciting texts: He talks like Laurence Olivier, a classical British actor, like Marlon Brando and like John Wayne.

- *Watch the sequence depicting Mr Keating's performance.*

- *Macbeth is about to murder the King of Scotland with a dagger. The knife appears to him as a vision.*
  Read the soliloquy and practise speaking it out loud.
  Imagine how Macbeth would feel at such a moment.
  Try out various ways of presenting the text to an audience.

IS THIS A DAGGER ...

Is this a dagger which I see before me,
The handle toward my hand? Come, let me clutch thee;
I have thee not, and yet I see thee still.
Art thou not, fatal vision, sensible
To feeling as to sight? Or art thou but
A dagger of the mind, a false creation,
Proceeding from the heat-oppressed brain?
I see thee yet, in form as palpable
As this which now I draw.
Thou marshall'st me the way that I was going;
And such an instrument I was to use.
Mine eyes are made the fools o' the other senses,
Or else worth all the rest. I see thee still;
And on thy blade and dudgeon gouts of blood,
Which was not so before. There's no such thing:
It is the bloody business which informs
Thus to mine eyes. Now o'er the one half-world
Nature seems dead, and wicked dreams abuse
The curtain'd sleep; now witchcraft celebrates
Pale Hecate's offerings; and wither'd murder,
Alarum'd by his sentinel, the wolf,
Whose howl's his watch, thus with his stealthy pace,
With Tarquin's ravishing strides, towards his design
Moves like a ghost ...

Macbeth, Act II, Scene 1

- *Compare the different ways the text can be spoken. Choose the one you like best.*

THE TEMPEST

Many years ago on a mystical isle, young Miranda and her loving father, Prospero, watched as a ship foundered in a fierce and terrible tempest. Prospero had been preparing for this moment for years, developing his magic powers from a rare book until he could control the elements. Miranda suspected that her father had caused the storm, but had no idea why such a gentle man should wish to harm anyone. So Prospero revealed how he and his daughter had been cast away on the island, twelve years before.

As the wise old bear once said, you're never too young for adventure.

For then thou wast not out three years old.	Thy father was the Duke of Milan.	Me, poor man, my library was dukedom large enough.	My brother, and thy uncle, call'd Antonio…	did believe he was indeed the duke.
The King of Naples… hearkens my brother's suit.	They hurried us aboard a barque;	bore us some leagues to sea.	Some food we had, and some fresh water.	Here in this island we arrived.

We like this, already.

Prospero had been Duke of Milan until his brother Antonio, aided by Alonso, King of Naples, seized power. Prospero and Miranda were set adrift in a tiny boat, but luckily a friend, Gonzalo, had secreted books and provisions on board. These sustained the pair until they drifted on to an island.

I bet he picks his nose.

When I was little, sprites were two a ducat!

The only inhabitants on this isle were the monster Caliban and the sprites his mother had trapped in trees before she died. Caliban became Prospero's servant, as did Ariel, an airy sprite. Ariel, who was invisible to all but Prospero, had been freed from a tree by Prospero's magic and in return had promised to serve him faithfully for twelve years.

Give us a posy.

Can you see Ariel?

No.

I think Ariel's hidden in the star.

You don't know nothing.

He's right.

Who's right?

I'm right. Ariel's just air.

Know-all.

By accident most strange, bountiful fortune, Now my dear lady, hath mine enemies Brought to this shore.

Prospero told Miranda that the storm-tossed ship carried his old enemies. Then, seeing Ariel approach, Prospero put a plan into action and sent Miranda to sleep.

But are they, Ariel, safe?

Not a hair perish'd... The king's son have I landed by himself.

Ariel spirited the ship's company ashore, isolating all but Antonio, Gonzalo and King Alonso. So the king feared that his son, Prince Ferdinand, must have drowned.

The thunder's over now, dearie.

Go, make thyself like to a nymph of the sea:

Ariel, now in the guise of a sea nymph, went to fetch Ferdinand to Prospero's cave.

Hag-seed, hence! Fetch us in fuel.

I must obey: his art is of such power.

Having dispatched Caliban to gather wood, Prospero then woke Miranda.

I might call him A thing divine.

O you wonder!

Full fathom five thy father lies.

Drawn to the cave by Ariel's singing, Ferdinand stared in wonder at lovely Miranda.

Potato?

...and hast put thyself upon this island as a spy.

No, as I am a man.

There's nothing ill can dwell in such a temple.

The two youngsters fell in love, as Prospero had planned. Adversity, he hoped, would seal the bond, so he accused Ferdinand of spying.

I'll manacle thy neck and feet together.

Beseech you, father!

He forbade Miranda to talk to Ferdinand and sent him to shift logs, which Ferdinand did willingly, to stay close to his beloved.

A little adversity does wonders for love.

Miranda, there are other men in the world.

I'll bear your logs the while.

No, precious creature.

For hours, Ferdinand hauled logs. Miranda never left his side.

Take my daughter.

Prospero watched Miranda and Ferdinand's love blossom, and finally he relented.

He conjured up a flock of nymphs to sing a blessing on their engagement.

PRIVATE BOX KEEP OUT

It's a sprite.

Lo now! Lo! I'll fall flat.

Meanwhile, Caliban gathered driftwood until a looming figure made him hide under his cloak.

Alas! The storm is come again.

It was Trinculo, King Alonso's jester who, fearing a storm, also crawled under the cloak.

This is some monster of the isle.

Minutes later, Stefano, the king's drunken butler, fell over the heaving bundle.

You're right there, you swiller!

Glug!

If they've been shipwrecked, why aren't they wet?

It's magic, stupids.

I think I can see Ariel.

Only Prospero can.

Antonio and King Alonso were awestruck into true repentance and begged to be forgiven. At last Prospero's anger was placated.

*Thy dukedom I resign, and do entreat
Thou pardon me my wrongs.*

Prospero released them from the circle and led them, and his old friend Gonzalo, to where Ferdinand and Miranda sat playing chess.

*If this prove
A vision of the island,
one dear son
Shall I twice lose.*

A happy ending!

Prospero's talking to himself again!

I chose her when I could not ask my father.

Let grief and sorrow still embrace his heart That doth not wish you joy!

Be it so! Amen!

Was't well done?

King Alonso was overjoyed at finding his son alive, and embraced him warmly. Ferdinand told the king of his wish to marry Miranda. Seeing Miranda's beauty and his son's happiness, King Alonso gave his consent. He hoped the union would heal the rift between Milan and Naples.

I think I'll stay in England.

I have been in such a pickle.

I am not Stefano, but a cramp.

I shall be pinch'd to death.

Go, sirrah, to my cell... trim it handsomely.

Into the midst of their rejoicing came Caliban, Trinculo and Stefano, urged on by Ariel. Prospero forgave them too, in return for a little hard labour. The party then made themselves comfortable, while Prospero recounted his adventures of the past twelve years.

Now my charms are all o'erthrown, And what strength I have's mine own.

They all planned to sail to Naples the next morning for the wedding of Miranda and Ferdinand, after which Prospero would return to Milan as its rightful duke. That night, Prospero released his faithful Ariel, who promised him fair winds for their journey. Then Prospero discarded his magic cloak, buried his staff deep in the ground and threw his book of magic out to sea. After twelve years Prospero was leaving the enchanted island to Caliban and the sprites. Prospero's tempest had served its purpose and his dukedom was restored.

From: Marcia Williams: *Mr William Shakespeare's Plays*, Walker Books Ltd. London 1988

- **Alonso, Antonio, Ariel, Caliban, Ferdinand, Gonzalo, Miranda, Prospero, Stefano, Trinculo:**
  Who are they? Explain in one or two sentences.

- *Retell the story in your own words. Divide the story into scenes.*

- *Prepare the different scenes in groups and replay them in class. Can you find some way to do the 'special effects'?*

- *Add your own commentary about the performance* ➜

There is a Scene Missing ...

In this part of the video Shakespeare explains the end of his play **Romeo and Juliet**. Everybody on the stage is moved until one of the actors notices that 'there is a scene missing' between marriage and death.

In fact Shakespeare writes this missing scene and you can see it later in the film or read it in **Romeo and Juliet**.

Will: For killing Juliet's kinsman Tybalt, the one who killed Romeo's friend Mercutio, Romeo is banished. But the Friar who married Romeo and Juliet ...

Edward: Is that me, Will?

Will: You Edward, the friar who married them gives Juliet a potion to drink. It is a secret potion. It makes us seeming dead. She is placed in the tomb of the Capulets. She will awake to life and love when Romeo comes to her side again. I have not said all. By maligned fate the message goes astray, which would tell Romeo of the friar's plan. He hears only that Juliet is dead. And thus he goes to the apothecary.

Fennyman: That's me.

Will: And buys a deadly poison. He enters the tomb to say farewell to Juliet, who lies there cold as death. He drinks the poison. He dies by her side. And then she wakes up and sees him dead. And so Juliet takes his dagger and kills herself.

Henslowe: Well, that will have them rolling in the aisles.

Fennyman: Sad ... and wonderful. I have a blue velvet cap that will do well. I have seen just such a cap on an apothecary. Just so.

Ned: Yes, it will serve. But there's a scene missing. Between marriage and death.

- *Watch the sequence on video.*

- *Work with one or two partners. Imagine what this missing scene could be like on the stage. Who would take part in it? Where will it be set? What might be going on? What would people say and do?*

- *Present your ideas by telling the class and/or by acting them out.*

- *Read the missing scene in Shakespeare's **Romeo and Juliet** (Act III, Scene 5). Read it aloud and act it out with a partner.*

- *Watch how it is depicted in the film.*

- *Compare Shakespeare's and the film's ideas with yours. Which do you prefer? Give reasons.*

shakespeare in Love

This sequence of the film **Shakespeare in Love** is set in the garden of the de Lesseps family. Viola is on the balcony of her room, her nurse inside is calling for her, William Shakespeare is in the garden below. For Viola and Will it is the very first time that they meet alone, almost alone.

Viola:	Romeo, Romeo, a young man of Verona, a comedy by William Shakespeare.
Nurse:	My lady!
Viola:	Who's there?
Shakespeare:	Will Shakespeare.
Nurse:	Madam!
Viola:	Anon, good nurse, anon. Master Shakespeare?
Shakespeare:	The same, alas.
Viola:	Why alas?
Shakespeare:	A lonely player!
Viola:	Alas indeed, I thought you the highest poet in my esteem, the writer of plays that capture my heart.
Shakespeare:	Oh, I am him, too.
Nurse:	Madam!
Viola:	Anon! I may come again.
Shakespeare:	Oh, I'm fortune's fool. I'll be punished for this. Oh my lady, my love.
Viola:	If they find you, they will kill you.
Shakespeare:	You could bring them with a word.
Viola:	Not for the world.
Nurse:	Madam!
Viola:	Anon!

anon bald, sogleich
alas ach, leider

At this moment Viola turns round and leaves the balcony to go into her room, from where the nurse is calling her. Shakespeare climbs up onto the balcony so that he can continue his conversation with Viola.

- *Discuss with two partners how you would act out this sequence.*
  One of you is the director, the other two are the actors.
  Practise reading the text, with different movements, gestures and facial expressions.
  Decide how you want to speak these sentences.

- *Play the scene and compare your presentation with others in the class.*

- *How do you think this conversation could continue? Where could it go?*
  Write down your ideas with a partner.
  Act them out before the class.
  Which ones do you like best? Can you give reasons?

- *Now watch how this sequence ends in the film.*

- *Which ending do you like better, yours or the one in the video? Give reasons.*

- *Homework: Write out the dialogue you developed in your team.*

On the Verona Balcony

ROMEO AND JULIET — Act II, Scene 2

Enter JULIET above at a window.

But, soft! What light through yonder
    window breaks?
It is the east, and Juliet is the sun.
Arise, fair sun, and kill the envious moon,
Who is already sick and pale with grief   5
That thou her maid art far more fair than
    she.
Be not her maid, since s
Her vestal livery is but
And none but fools do w
It is my lady; O, it is m
O that she knew she wer
She speaks, yet she says
    that?
Her eye discourses; I wi
I am too bold, 'tis not to
Two of the fairest stars
Having some business, d
To twinkle in their spher
What if her eyes were
    head?
The brightness of her ch
    those stars,
As daylight doth a lan
    heaven
Would through the airy
    bright
That birds would sing,
    not night.
See how she leans her che
O that I were a glove up
That I might touch that
    Jul.
    Rom.
O, speak again, bright a
As glorious to this nigh
    head,
As is a winged messenge
Unto the white-upturned
Of mortals that fall back
When he bestrides the la
And sails upon the boson
    Jul. O Romeo, Rom
    thou Romeo?
Deny thy father and ref
Or, if thou wilt not, be but sworn my love,
And I'll no longer be a Capulet.
    Rom. [*Aside*] Shall I hear more, or shall
    I speak at this?
    Jul. 'Tis but thy name that is my enemy;
Thou art thyself, though not a Montague.
What's Montague? It is nor hand, nor
    foot,
Nor arm, nor face, nor any other part   40
Belonging to a man. O, be some other
    name!
What's in a name? That which we call a
    rose
By any other name would smell as sweet;
So Romeo would, were he not Romeo
    call'd,   45
Retain that dear perfection which he owes

Without that title. Romeo, doff thy name;
And for thy name, which is no part of thee,
Take all myself.
    Rom.   I take thee at thy word:
Call me but love, and I'll be new baptiz'd;
Henceforth I never will be Romeo.   51
    Jul. What man art thou, that, thus be-
    screen'd in night
...
...   56
...rd.
...nk a
...w the
...e?   60
...thee
...e, and
...rd to
...thou
...   65
...o'er-
...t;
...love
...o me.
...urder
...   70
...thine
...swords; look thou
...t their enmity.
...the world they saw
...s clo
...s;
...e, let
My life were better ended
Than death prorogued want
    Jul. By whose direction
    out this place?
    Rom. By love, that first
    to enquire;
He lent me counsel, and I
I am no pilot; yet, wert
As that vast shore wash'd
    sea,
I should adventure for su
    Jul. Thou knowest the
    on my face,
Else would a maiden b
    cheek
For that which thou has
    to-night.

> • How could Shakespeare present his balcony scene
>   in a modern film version?
>   Get together in groups of three – Romeo, Juliet,
>   film director – and discuss / try out your ideas.
>
>   How did John Madden, director of **Shakespeare in
>   Love**, do it? Watch the film.

"Romeo, Romeo,
Are you on line, Romeo?"

A 'Sugared' Sonnet

SONNET 18

Shall I compare thee to a summer's day?
Thou art more ░░░░░░░ and more ░░░░░░
░░░░░ winds do shake the Darling buds of May,
And summer's lease hath all too ░░░░░░ a date:

Sometime too ░░░░░░░ the eye of heaven shines,
And often is his ░░░░░░ complexion dimm'd;
And every fair from fair sometime declines,
By chance or nature's ░░░░░░░ course untrimm'd;

But thy ░░░░░░ summer shall not fade,
Nor lose possession of that fair thou ow'st;
Nor shall Death brag thou wander'st in his shade,
When in eternal lines to time thou grow'st:

So long as men can ░░░░░░░ or eyes can see,
So long lives this, and this gives ░░░░░░░ to thee.

beautiful
lovely
cold   stormy
hope
Changing   eternal
short
breathe   rough
pleasant   sweet
red
life   gold
hot
pretty   red
temperate
stormy
cold

> eternal lines in a poem
> to time thou grow'st you stay alive

- *Decide with a partner which words from the Love list make sense in the text of the sonnet.*
- *Present your results by reading your version out to your class. Compare and discuss the different versions.*
- *Compare your version with the original sonnet.*
- *Do you believe alternative versions of the poem are also acceptable?*
- *Recite the sonnet in your class.*

Shakespeare's English is so difficult to understand!

Think about pronunciation, intonation, expression, speed, rhythm ... !!

Isn't it stupid to read poetry which is over 400 years old?

- *Schoolmaster Francis Meres called Shakespeare's sonnets 'sugared'. Can you imagine why?*

> '... the sweete wittie soule of Ouid lives in mellifluous hony-tongued Shakespeare, witness his
> *Venus and Adonis*, his *Lucrece*, his sugred Sonnets among his private friends, ...'

What's a Sonnet??

A sonnet is a poem with 14 lines, each containing 10 or 11 syllables, and a fixed scheme. **The Italian sonetto** derived from *sonare* (to sound) and became very popular when Petrarch (1304 – 1374) wrote 327 sonnets about the life and death of Madonna Laura.

The English sonnet is also called **Shakespearean sonnet** because Shakespeare's 154 sonnets were the most popular. They are usually arranged in three *quatrains* (four-liners) and a *couplet*, rhyming abab cdcd efef gg and written in *iambic pentameter*.

Thus the English sonnet may give three examples – one in each *quatrain* – and draw a conclusion (the final statement) in the *couplet*.

The traditional topic of sonnets is love, and sonnet sequences such as those by Petrarch and Shakespeare form a related series of lyrical explorations on love or friendship, betrayed love, love renewed, etc.

- *Cut out the 14 lines of Sonnet 130. Arrange them in the right order.*

Than in the breath that from my mistress reeks; ✂

If hairs be wires, black wires grow on her head.

I have seen roses damask'd, red and white,

SONNET 130

Coral is far more red than her lips' red;

a
b
a
b

c
d
c
d

e
f
e
f

g
g

As any she belied with false compare.

But no such roses see I in her cheeks;

That music hath a far more pleasing sound;

I love to hear her speak, yet well I know

I grant I never saw a goddess go –

And yet, by heaven, I think my love as rare

My mistress when she walks treads on the ground.

And in some perfumes is there more delight

If snow be white, why then her breasts are dun;

My mistress' eyes are nothing like the sun;

Listen to Your Heart Beat

Yeah, I liked the play. It was just the language that was a bit strange.

SO FOUL AND FAIR A DAY I HAVE NOT SEEN.

Most of the time Shakespeare wrote in verses like this.

Each line has ten syllables, every second one is stressed.

• *Use your desk as a drum and beat the rhythm while you speak the line several times.*

Sounds quite boring after a while, doesn't it?
Shakespeare found ways of making his verse more interesting.

This is what King Henry V tells his soldiers before a battle against the French. The English are exhausted and afraid, the French have got five times more soldiers and are well rested:

Earl of Westmoreland:
                              O that we now had here
But one ten thousand of those men in England
That do no work to-day!

Henry V: What's he that wishes so?
My cousin Westmoreland? No, my fair cousin:
If we are mark'd to die, we are enow
To do our country loss; and if to live,
The fewer men, the greater share of honour.
God's will! I pray thee, wish not one man more.
[...]
Rather proclaim it, Westmoreland, through my host,
That he which hath no stomach to this fight,
Let him depart; his passport shall be made,
And crowns for convoy put into his purse;
We would not die in that man's company
That fears his fellowship to die with us.
[...]
We few, we happy few, we band of brothers;
For he to-day that sheds his blood with me
Shall be my brother; be he ne'er so vile,
This day shall gentle his condition;
And gentlemen in England now a-bed
Shall think themselves accurs'd they were not here ...

King Henry V, Act IV, Scene 3

• *Speak the lines aloud. First to yourself, then to a partner.
Remember: King Henry has to be very enthusiastic and convincing so his soldiers won't turn on him and run away. Concentrate on the sense, not on the form of the text.*

• *Shakespeare uses mainly one technique here to break up the strict rhythm. Check the info box to find out which one.*

Shakespeare's Verse

The length of the line is counted in stresses and determines the **metre**.
A typical Shakespearean line has ten syllables:
– every other one is stressed (that makes it a **iambus**)
– as there are ten syllables, five are stressed (that makes it a **pentameter**)
→ Shakespeare uses **iambic pentameter** most of the time.

Although the rhythm comes very close to our natural rhythm of speech, it might sound monotonous after a while. To break up the *iambic pentameter* Shakespeare often doesn't end his sentences at the end of a line, but lets them run into the next line (**run-on lines or enjambement**). Sometimes he even divides one line between two speakers. The best way to avoid sounding boring is to concentrate on the sense – the rest comes naturally.
By the way: *-ed* at the end of a verb was pronounced as a complete syllable [ɪd]. If there were too many syllables in a line, then Shakespeare would cut the [ɪ] and mark it with an apostrophe (*bestow'd, wither'd*).

The lines don't necessarily have to rhyme. It sounds more natural if they don't. So Shakespeare mostly writes without rhyme. In other words: his verses are *blank*.
→ **blank verse**
Exceptions are the ends of scenes. To signal the audience a change Shakespeare often ends scenes with two rhyming lines or
→ **heroic couplets**
Shakespeare wasn't the man to be pressed into a strict form. He used iambic pentameter when it seemed natural to him. He changed the pattern when it seemed necessary. Usually he had his kings, queens, noblemen and noblewomen speak about great and tragic topics in verse while servants, clowns and madmen spoke prose.
→ *No rule without exception*

> THE TIME IS OUT OF JOINT, O CURSED SPITE,
> THAT EVER I WAS BORN TO SET IT RIGHT! –

• *You will find these two lines in* Hamlet, *Act I, Scene 5.*
  Where in this scene would you expect to find them and why?
  Check the info box for the answer.

Will's Words

Many of William Shakespeare's words are no longer used in modern English, or they have a different meaning. Here is a list of the most common ones:

(to) **affect** sb	an jdm Gefallen finden, jdn vorziehen
(to) **affright** sb	jdn erschrecken, jdm Angst machen
alarum	Getümmel
ally	Verwandter
(to) **avouch** sth	etw behaupten, bekräftigen
aweary of sth	einer Sache überdrüssig
beaver	Visier, Helmsturz
bedfellow	Bettgenosse, Schlafkamerad
(to) **beshrew** sb/sth	jdn/etw verfluchen
(to) **bespeak** sb (bespoke, bespoken)	jdn ansprechen, anreden
(to) **bethink** one(self) of sth (bethought, bethought)	sich an etw erinnern
(to) **betide** sb	jdm geschehen, widerfahren
blazon	Schilderung, Darstellung
brake	Dickicht
brave	fein, prächtig
bravery	Pracht
broil	Zank, Streit
(to) **brook** sth	etw ertragen
choler	Zorn
(to) **keep** sth **close**	etw geheim halten
clout	Lappen
coil	Tumult, Durcheinander
mortal **coil**	Mühsal des Irdischen
continent	Gefäß, Behälter
(to) **cope** sb	jdm begegnen
(to) **counterfeit** (sth)	sich verstellen; (etw) vortäuschen
coxcomb	Stutzer; Narrenkappe; Kopf
(to) **cozen** sb (of sth)	jdn (um etw) betrügen, täuschen
dam	*abwertend* für: Mutter
darkling	im Dunkeln
(to) **deliver** sb	jdn befreien, erlösen
sth **dislikes** sb	etw missfällt jdm
distemper	Krankheit, Leiden;
(to) ~ sb/sth	jdn/etw stören
(to) **doff** sth	etw ablegen
dole	Kummer, Plage
durance; in ~	Haft; in Haft
(to) **enfranchise** sb	jdn befreien
(to) **enlarge** sb	jdn freilassen
fell	fürchterlich, grausam
(to) **fleer** at sth	etw verspotten
front	Stirn
(to) **gall** sb	jdn ärgern, reizen
gamesome	lebenslustig
gaud	Flitter, Schmuckstück
(to) **gin** (gan, gun)	beginnen
(to) **glister**	glänzen, glitzern
gossip	Gevatterin
gull	Gimpel, Tölpel
(to) **gull** sb	jdn reinlegen, betrügen
(to) **gyve** sb	jdn fesseln
gyves (Plural)	Fesseln
hap	Glück; geschehen
harness	Harnisch
hight	genannt
invention	Fantasie; Schöpfung
knavish	schalkhaft, schelmisch
(to) **lie** (lay, lain)	schlafen, übernachten
(to) **lie** with sb	mit jdm übernachten; mit jdm schlafen
(to) **list**	zuhören
(to) **list** sb	jdn gelüsten, jdm belieben
(to) **mend**	sich bessern
(to) **mew** (up) sb	jdn einsperren
minion	Liebling, Günstling; Geliebte
(to) **miscarry**	sterben
(to) **misgive** that …	befürchten, dass …
the **morrow**:	der nächste Tag
good ~	guten Morgen
(to) make **mouths**	Grimassen schneiden
(to) **owe** sth	etw haben, besitzen
(to) **palter** with sb	mit jdm tändeln, mit jdm sein Spiel treiben
part	weggehen
parts (*pl*)	(geistige) Fähigkeiten
perpend	gib acht
physic	Heilkunde, Medizin; Arznei
(to) **physic** sb	jdn ärztlich behandeln
poniard	Dolch
points (*pl*)	Schnüre zum Befestigen der Beinkleider
powers (*pl*)	Heer
pox	Syphilis
(to) **prick** sb	jdn (aus einer Liste) auswählen
(to) **prick** sb on	jdn antreiben
(to) **rate** sb	jdn ausschelten, ausschimpfen
revels (*pl*)	Vergnügungen, Lustbarkeiten
(to) **rive** sth (rived, riven)	etw spalten
rude	von niedriger Herkunft
wise **saws**	weise Sprüche
shaft; **love-shaft**	Pfeil; Liebespfeil
sooth	Wahrheit

sport; to make **sport**	Tändelei, angenehmer Zeitvertreib; sich belustigen
(to) **stay** sb/sth	jdn/etw aufhalten
(to) **stint**	aufhören
stoup	Becher
strange	reserviert, zurückhaltend
(to) be **suited**	bekleidet sein
(to) **swinge** sb	jedn durchprügeln, (aus)peitschen
tabor	Handtrommel
tall	kühn, mutig
(to) **tarry** for sth; ~ somewhere	auf etw warten; irgendwo bleiben
twain	zwei
twelvemonth	Jahr
undone	ruiniert; zugrunde gerichtet
visage	Antlitz, angesicht
visor	Maske
wanton	Tändler, Schelm
weed	Kleidungsstück, Gewand
welkin	Himmel, Firmament
whoreson	Bankert, Bastard; gemein, niedrig
wittol	Hahnrei
wood	rasend, wahnsinnig
ycleped/yclept	genannt, namens

❋ Redewendungen und Ausdrücke

anon anon	ich komme sofort
what **boots** it?	was nützt es?
commend me to my brother	empfehle mich meinem Bruder
by my **faith**!	wahrlich, meiner Treu!
at one **fell** swoop	auf einen Schlag
fie	pfui, schäm dich
I am not gamesome	ich habe keine Lust am Spiel
go to	hör auf
(to) catch sb upon the **hip**	jdn an seiner schwachen Stelle angreifen
this **likes** me well	das gefällt mir gut
marry!	fürwahr!
(to) think **meet** to do sth	es für angemessen halten, etw zu tun
I cry you **mercy**	es tut mir Leid
methinks (methought, methought)	mich dünkt, mir scheint
(to) **say** sb **nay**	jdm nein sagen
what's thy **pleasure**?	was wünschst du?
pox	verflucht!
prithee	bitte/ich bitte dich
save thee/you	Gott grüß dich
sirrah	he du, du Bursche
in **sooth**	wahrhaftig, wahrlich

by my **troth**!	meiner Treu, wahrlich
zounds!	sapperlot!, verflucht!

❋ Grammatische Wörter

❋ Verben

art	(du) bist
wast	(du) warst
beest	(du) seist
wert	(du) wärst
dost	(du) tust
doth	(er/sie/es) tut
hast	(du) hast
hath	(er/sie/es) hat

❋ Präpositonen

ere	vor
ere this	zuvor, vorher
thorough	durch
withal	mit

❋ Pronomen

a, a'	er

❋ Konjunktionen

an	wenn
ere	ehe, bevor

❋ Adverbien

anon	bald
aright	zu Recht
for **aye**	für immer
belike	vielleicht, wahrscheinlich
betimes	früh; beizeiten
eke	auch
even now	vor kurzen
haply	vielleicht
hard by	ganz in der Nähe
incontinent(ly)	sofort
ne'er	nie
passing	äußerst, sehr
withal	außerdem, dazu

Aus: *Pons – Wörterbuch für Schule und Studium*, Stuttgart 2001

THOU PUKING BOIL-BRAINED HORN-BEAST

Never use one word when two or more will do …
Elizabethan English was – and had to be – a rather colourful language.

If you want to learn some Elizabethan, …

bootless
impertinent
goatish
infectious
weedy
puking
spongy
vain
villainous
vended

boil-brained
fool-born
onion-eyed
fat-kidneyed
doghearted
milk-livered
dizzy-eyed
fly-bitten
beetle-headed
hell-hated

boar-pig
bladder
foot-licker
horn-beast
pignut
wagtail
malt-worm
hedge-pig
baggage
maggot-pie

… try insults

- To make a really worthwhile insult:
→ Take one word from each cape.
→ Start your insult with 'thou' (meaning 'you').
→ Now speak it to your partner, with all the expression that you can

– and run in case your partner understands!

In case you want to be nice:

Elizabethan society was very class-orientated. You had to be careful how to address somebody you didn't know. Luckily a person's clothes would tell you all you needed to know:

- *How did people address each other?*
  Complete the puzzle, then you'll know.

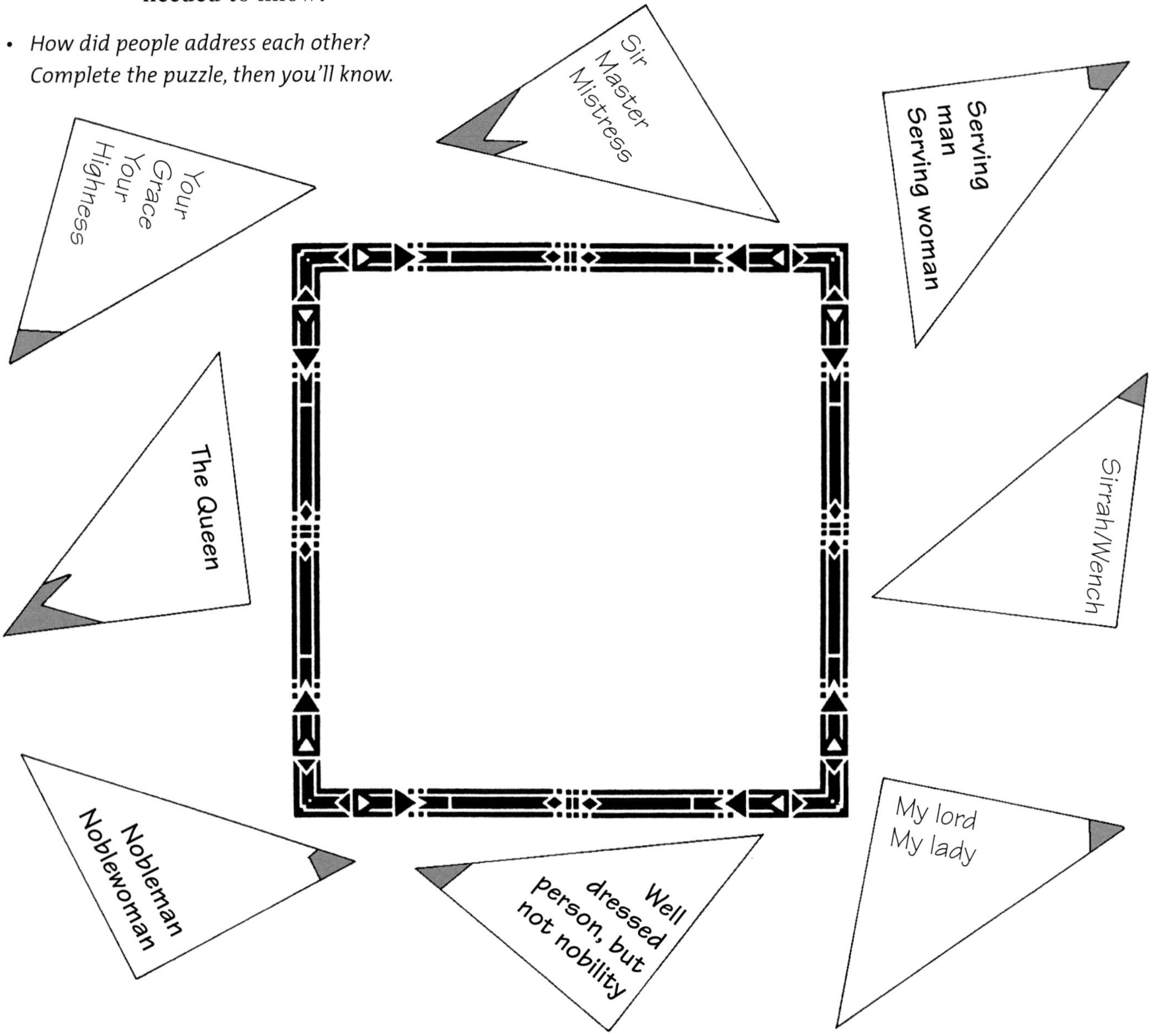

Your Grace
Your Highness

Sir
Master
Mistress

Serving man
Serving woman

The Queen

Sirrah/Wench

Nobleman
Noblewoman

Well dressed person, but not nobility

My lord
My lady

Make very short dialogues in Elizabethan English with your partner.
Try them out loud.

thou du · **alarum** Getümmel · **bedfellow** Bettgenosse · **broil** Streit · **clout** Lappen **continent** Gefäß · **dole** Kummer · **gull** Tölpel **invention** Fantasie · **minion** Geliebte · **poniard** Dolch · **revels** Vergnügen · **visage** Gesicht **weed** Gewand

tall mutig · **undone** ruiniert · **fell** grausam **gamesome** lebenslustig **vile** von niedriger Herkunft

belike wahrscheinlich · **betimes** rechtzeitig **HARD BY** ganz nah · **WITHAL** außerdem

art bist · **wast** warst · **dost** tust · **hast** hast **to affright sb.** jmd. erschrecken · **to avouch sth.** etwas behaupten · **to keep sth. close** etw. geheimhalten · **to counterfeit** etwas vortäuschen · **to gall sb.** jmd. ärgern **to gull sb.** jmd. betrügen · **to make mouths** Grimassen schneiden · **to winge sb.** jmd. prügeln

commend me empfehlen Sie mich · **go to** hör auf · **methinks** ich glaube · **prithee** ich bitte dich · **anon** komme gleich

Acting is ...

There, there. Let me pull the covers up around you, sweetheart. That's it. Now gently close your eyes. Everything's okay. Try and ignore what's going on downstairs, darling. Just let it all drift away. Shhh. Think of all the wonderful things you'll be doing tomorrow. All the new adventures you'll be having ...

Have they lost their nerve, I wonder? The ref is looking nervous. And the whistle goes for the second half. Deakin now defiant. Let's hope they've been thinking hard over half-time. Jones has possession. Evans is moving into position. Oh, and Hatchett has tackled it away from him. And he's off! What a player! The crowd is going wild!

Hanley! Brooks! Cookson! Finally decided to put in an appearance, eh? Right. Down you go. Forty press-ups! Starting NOW! Let's see some more enthusiasm, Brooks. Come on, Hanley. Nose to the ground. And fifteen, sixteen, seventeen. Faster, Brooks. Keep that back straight. And thirty-nine, forty. On your feet. Now get a move on and join the others on the exercise ground.

Fillet of a fenny snake,
In the cauldron boil and bake:
Eye of newt, and toe of frog,
Wool of bat, and tongue of dog,
Adder's fork, and blind worm's sting,
Lizard's leg, and owlet's wing,
For a charm of powerful trouble
Like a hell-broth boil and bubble.

Double, double toil and trouble;
Fire burn, and cauldron bubble.

- *Match the texts to the photos.*
- *Pick one of the texts and prepare it so you can read it aloud in front of the class.*
  The other students should be able to get a picture of your character without understanding the whole text.
  Pay attention to things like speed, pauses, volume, hard or soft tone of voice, etc.

using your voice

Acting is ...

• *Together with a partner try out some of the gestures and find a suitable translation for the Latin description.*

You don't have any knowledge of Latin?
What does the gesture feel like when you perform it?
Yes, that's the answer.
Don't worry, if you can't figure out all 24.

Fear, excitement, anger, exhaustion ...

• *Try to portray these emotions without saying a word.*

Changing a baby's nappies, cleaning windows, putting up a tent, trying to get a motor-bike started ...

• *Act out these situations without talking. Let the other students guess what you are doing.*

The gestures of actors of the seventeenth century, from: Bulwer's *Chirologia*, London, 1644

using your body

Acting is merely ...

The text of a play is just a skeleton.
Here are some suggestions how to put flesh on it:

Step ❶: Pick a scene you like.
→ Read it in class, so you basically know what it is all about.

Step ❷: Talk about how to prepare the stage.
→ Use tables and chairs and possibly drape them with cloths (old curtains, sheets, etc.).
→ Decide which props might help the understanding of the text and where to get them (sticks for swords, dark balsamico vinegar for blood (if you like it less smelly use a thin red cloth for blood), letters, a skull, a knife, flowers, books …).

Step ❸: Which background noises would help?
→ Can some sort of background music be used?
→ Can you produce some sounds (violently move a large metal sheet for thunder, clap coconut shells for horses, put the tip of a pipe in a bowl of water and blow for bird song …)?
→ Are recordings available (bell, clock, chimes …)?

Step ❹: Is it possible to use costumes?
In Elizabethan times costumes were very elaborate to impress the audience. As there was hardly any scenery on stage costumes were very important.
→ It might be more practical to use no costumes and only give each character some distinguishing mark (a crown for a king, a cape for a nobleman, a piece of armour for a knight, long skirt/curtain wrapped around the waist for a lady …)
→ Make paper masks that cover the upper part of the character's face and decorate them accordingly (glue leaves, flowers and moss onto the mask for elves …).

Step ❺: Prepare the text.
→ Write down the text for each character on a separate piece of paper. The actors learn their lines at home and then rehearse individually with a partner in class before the different parts are put together.
→ If it's a complicated scene, an outline of the plot is written and pinned to the wall as a basic guideline.

Step ❻: Check that everyone has got a task.
→ actors, prop-boys/girls, lighting technicians, prompters, director, bookkeeper

Step ❼: Go!
Remember the stage crew in Shakespeare's times usually had about three to four days to rehearse a complete play. They often didn't know the whole text and concentrated on their part only. So have a go and try to make sense of your scene for yourself. Then your acting will certainly be …

the art of keeping a large group of people from coughing.

Ralph Richardson

THERE'S SMALL CHOICE

PICK THE TWO

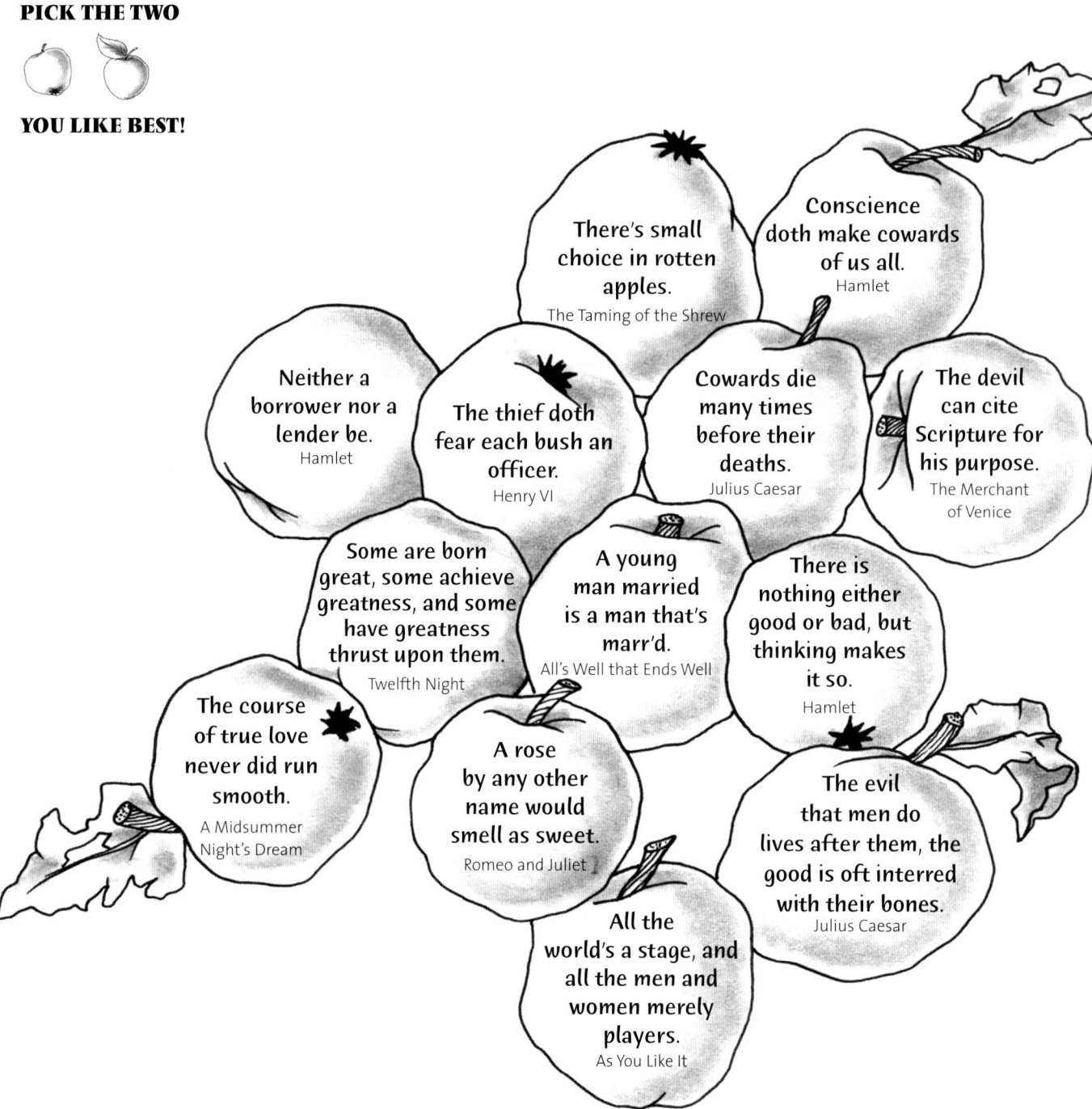

YOU LIKE BEST!

There's small choice in rotten apples.
The Taming of the Shrew

Conscience doth make cowards of us all.
Hamlet

Neither a borrower nor a lender be.
Hamlet

The thief doth fear each bush an officer.
Henry VI

Cowards die many times before their deaths.
Julius Caesar

The devil can cite Scripture for his purpose.
The Merchant of Venice

Some are born great, some achieve greatness, and some have greatness thrust upon them.
Twelfth Night

A young man married is a man that's marr'd.
All's Well that Ends Well

There is nothing either good or bad, but thinking makes it so.
Hamlet

The course of true love never did run smooth.
A Midsummer Night's Dream

A rose by any other name would smell as sweet.
Romeo and Juliet

The evil that men do lives after them, the good is oft interred with their bones.
Julius Caesar

All the world's a stage, and all the men and women merely players.
As You Like It

- *Decide on a way to present the concrete meaning of your chosen* 🍎 🍎 *proverbs to your class. You might want*
    - ➔ *to draw a picture that explains them on a transparency;*
    - ➔ *to perform a mime with your partner.*
    - **???** *You are free to try whatever makes sense!*

- *Discuss the meaning with your partner and then tell the class.*

IN ROTTEN APPLES

Shakespeare's 'German Proverbs'

Shakespeare's works have frequently been translated into German and have always been very popular in Germany.
So several quotations or sayings are also known or even used in our country.

Frailty, thy name is woman!
Hamlet

Let me have men about me that are fat.
Julius Caesar

He thinks too much; such men are dangerous.
Julius Caesar

The time is out of joint.
Hamlet

This was a man!
Julius Caesar

To be, or not to be: that is the question.
Hamlet

Something is rotten in the state of Denmark.
Hamlet

There are more things in heaven and earth Horatio Than are dreamt of in your philosophy.
Hamlet

A horse! a horse! My kingdom for a horse!
Richard III

Ay, every inch a king.
King Lear

The tooth of time
Measure for Measure

Love's labour's lost

Come what come may
Macbeth

Much ado about nothing

The rest is silence.
Hamlet

- *Try to translate the proverbs into German.*

Do you recognize the 'German' proverbs?

Komme, was kommen mag.
Verlorne Liebesmüh
Viel Lärm um nichts
Der Rest ist Schweigen.

Die Zeit ist aus den Fugen.
Sein oder Nichtsein, das ist hier die Frage.
Ein Pferd! Ein Pferd! Ein Königreich für ein Pferd!
Jeder Zoll ein König!
Der Zahn der Zeit

Schwachheit, dein Name ist Weib!
Dies war ein Mann!
Lasst wohlbeleibte Männer um mich sein.
Er denkt zuviel, die Leute sind gefährlich.
Es gibt mehr Ding' im Himmel und auf Erden,
als eure Schulweisheit sich träumen lässt.
Etwas ist faul im Staate Dänemark.

REINVENTION OF WINTER

When icicles hang by the wall,
1. And Dick the shepherd _____
2. And Tom _____ into the hall,
   And milk comes frozen home in pail;
3. When _____, and ways be foul,
4. Then _____ the staring owl:
   Tu-whoo!
   Tu-whit, tu-whoo! – a merry note,
5. While _____

6. When all aloud _____
7. And coughing _____
8. And birds sit _____ the snow,
9. And Marian's _____ looks red and raw;
10. When _____ in the bowl,
11. Then _____ the staring owl:
    Tu-whoo!
    Tu-whit, tu-whoo! – a merry note,
12. While _____

From: *Love's Labour's Lost*, Act V, Scene 2

- Even the world's best-known author turned his attention to simpler things like seasonal songs or poems.
  Here is your challenge: Try to complete the lines as you think best to create your winter poem.
  Perhaps you will hit on the right words and be a natural to succeed Mr Shakespeare!

1 blows his nail, •hides from hail, •shuns the dale
2 drives dogs, •serves grogs, •bears logs

3 tea is sipped, •blood is nipped, •hose be ripped
4 sprightly wings, •nightly sings, •brightly winks

5 dizzy Ron doth reel and dote. •squeezy Mona's full of snot. •greasy Joan doth keel the pot.

6 the cock cries snow, •the ice doth groan, •the wind doth blow

7 sounds in every maw, •drowns the parson's saw, •seems the winter's law
8 brooding in, •freezing from, •silent on
9 face •nose, •breast
10 roasted crabs hiss, •brindled cats feast, •crazed rats scratch
11 sprightly wings, •nightly sings, •brightly winks

12 dizzy Ron doth reel and dote. •sqeezy Mona's full of snot. •greasy Joan doth keel the pot.

Shakespeare and Myself

The first English writer whom I came to know intimately was William Shakespeare. I myself am the second.

There are certain differences between us which – in spite of the many books written about Shakespeare – have not been pointed out with sufficient clarity. He was born at Stratford-upon-Avon, in the County of
5 Warwick (England); I was born in Siklos, in the County of Baranya (Hungary). Very few outstanding English writers were born in Siklos – but not too many were born at Stratford, either.

As a successful English playwright, Shakespeare was second only to Ivor Novello. If I compare him with myself, however, – which seems inevitable – I find that almost all relevant points are in my favour. First, he wrote in archaic English which is often tiresome, while my language is absolutely up to the minute. (He
10 cannot be blamed for this because he learned English earlier than I did; he was two when he learned it; I was 25.) Secondly, as a humorist, he belonged to rather a low class. He was a punster and he kept on cracking jokes. Cracking jokes should be below the dignity of any humorist who thinks something of himself. Jokes may be all right in tragedies and in any other kind of gloomy literature which needs light relief but they are quite out of place in serious humour. Thirdly, he was a hack. He turned out one play after the other for the
15 commercial theatre, which kept him away from the kind of writing he was really keen on. 'Business is business,' he sighed bitterly and sat down to write Hamlet. He, like all sensitive souls, preferred cash to fame. But he acquired more fame than cash and that rankled more and more as he grew older.

The parallel between Shakespeare and myself, however, can be stretched too far. We are different kinds of writers. He was a playwright, I am a travel-book writer. He was always on the look-out for a soft job. He wrote
20 about people of the past, people of ancient Rome and faraway Verona who presented no difficulties because nobody knew them. But I write about the English, who are unfathomable and keep perplexing. It was easy for Shakespeare.

Very little is known about our lives. It is characteristic of the
25 English that they turn out innumerable books on the life of Shakespeare – about whom it is almost impossible to find out anything – but
30 not one single volume has been written about me, although I am just round the corner.

[...]

George Mikes: *Shakespeare and Myself*. Introduction. In: George Mikes: How to be a Yank and More Wisdom. Harmondsworth: Penguin Books 1989, pp. 223 f.

What about Shakespeare and yourself?

* *Can you imagine why Shakespeare is considered so 'great' and 'important' that people call him 'the best writer of all times'? What do* **YOU** *think about him?*
* *Would you like to add yourself to the cartoon?*
* *What (perhaps humorous) remarks about Shakespeare and yourself can you think of?*

THE UNIVERSAL SHAKESPEARE

> Ah, Captain Spock, you have never experienced Shakespeare until you have read him in the original Klingon.
>
> J. M. Dillard: *Star Trek II - The Undiscovered Country*, p. 78

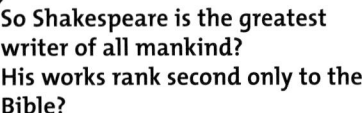

THE KLINGON CHANCELLOR GORKON

**So Shakespeare is the greatest writer of all mankind?
His works rank second only to the Bible?
The most famous Englishman in the world?
Do you really believe this?
If you have doubts, listen to this:**

CAPTAIN SPOCK

Wil'yam Shex' pir is a figure of vital importance in Klingon culture. He was an astute observer of both Klingon character and Klingon politics. It has rightly been said that it is impossible for an alien to appreciate who Klingons really are, unless they have come to understand Shex'pir. At a time when relations between the Federation and the Empire have reached a certain degree of normalization, and when citizens of the Federation are increasingly seeking to know more about Klingons and their way of life, we are satisfied to present this work [a Klingon edition of *Hamlet*, Anm. d.Vf.] as a contribution towards better understanding and respect between our two races. ...

It is regrettable that, during the years when the Empire and Federation were at war, certain individuals resorted to crude forgeries of Shex'pir, claiming him as a conveniently remote medieval Terran, a certain Willem Shekispeore, and hoping by this falsification of history to discredit the achievements of Klingon culture. [...]
This has had the interesting side-effect that passages in the two plays, pretty much identical textually, are interpreted in wildly differing ways by the two cultures. The differences between how *Khamlet* is read on Earth and Kronos are an excellent illustration of the different values of Klingon and Federation society; and a careful examination of this should prove rewarding to anyone interested in understanding Klingons better. [...]

To come to this particular play: Khamlet is widely regarded amongst Klingons as a problematic play. This is because of the daring innovations by Shex'pir on the conventions of the genre of the revenge play (**bortaS lut**). In the Klingon tradition of the revenge play, *Khamlet* would have been a simple affair: Klaw'diyush should have been dispatched with little ceremony ten minutes into the play. This does not occur. Instead, Khamlet spends a positively un-Klingon amount of time talking about what he should do, rather than getting anything done. Most Klingons cannot make head or tail of this; in some parts of the hinterlands of the Empire, Khamlet has even been

banned from performance, as liable to corrupt the youth.
The disparities between Klingon and Federation culture are such that it is usually when Federation audiences think 'Amlet' is mad that Klingon audiences think he has momentarily come to his senses. Such instances include the murder of Polonyush, Khamlet's overt flirting with Ovelya, and – as some of his soliloquies. A good illustration of these cultural disparities lies in Act III Scene 1. For both Klingon and Federation audiences, something about the scene does not make sense; Khamlet/Amlet starts acting in an inexplicable manner, and to explain this it is usually assumed that he has caught a glimpse of the King and Polonyush spying on him, and he changes his behaviour to play up to them accordingly. In the Terran version, this turn in his actions comes right after his soliloquy, when he coldly dismisses Ofelea. To Klingons, his behaviour against the suddenly meek, apologetic Ovelya makes all the sense in the world. What doesn't make sense is the preceding soliloquy, which is explained by Klingon scholars as Khamlet giving the King and Polonyush what they want – a 'mad' Khamlet – although there is enough meaning and honor left in the speech that the King and Polonyush are not fooled.
It has caused Klingon social analysts no end of mirth to realize how highly Terrans prize the *To be or not to be* soliloquy; if Klingons had to single out one soliloquy above all others, it would be *Tis now the very witching time of night*, at the end of III 2, a speech which expresses the Klingon drive towards revenge masterfully. [...]

But it is important to bear in mind that *Khamlet's* soliloquies are not intended as tomfoolery or slapstick – though the Act III Scene 1 soliloquy in particular is often performed as such. Their premise is sound enough that they won't be instantly rejected by a Klingon audience; it is their tendency to belabour the point, and to go on just a bit too long, that succeed in causing a deep feeling of unease.

There are many other illuminating parts of the play which we will let the Federation reader uncover himself. Read this work, Human, and learn.

From: Nick Nicholas, Introduction to: *Hamlet – The Restored Version*, Flourtown, PA: Klingon Language Institute, 1996

- *Inform yourself about Klingon culture. Why is Hamlet called an un-Klingon play?
  Collect reasons and compare them with a partner.*

- *Compare the Klingon view with our Terran view of Hamlet's actions. Should Hamlet have killed Claudius earlier?
  Why is he reluctant to kill him? Does his hestitating make sense to you?*

To be, or not to be: that is the question –

Whether 'tis nobler in the mind to suffer
The slings and arrows of outrageous fortune,
Or to take arms against a sea of troubles,
And, by opposing, end them? To die, to sleep –
No more; and by a sleep to say we end
The heart-ache and the thousand natural shocks
That flesh is heir to. 'Tis a consummation
Devoutly to be wished. To die, to sleep –
To sleep, perchance to dream … ay, there's the rub,
For in that sleep of death what dreams may come,
When we have shuffled off this mortal coil,
Must give us pause. …

Hamlet, Act III, Scene 1

'Tis now the very witching time of night,

When churchyards yawn, and hell itself breathes out
Contagion to this world. Now could I drink hot blood,
And do such bitter business as the day
Would quake to look on … Soft! Now to my mother –
O heart, lose not thy nature, let not ever
The soul of Nero enter this firm bosom.
Let me be cruel, not unnatural;
I will speak daggers to her, but use none.
My tongue and soul in this be hypocrites –
How in my words somever she be shent,
To give them seals never, my soul, consent!

Hamlet, Act III, Scene 2

INFO: Star Trek and the Klingon Culture

The TV series *Star Trek* has achieved cult-like status throughout the last 30 years. It basically tells of the travels of a spaceship from earth (*Enterprise*) through the galaxies where its crew encounters many different cultures. The time is supposed to be the 23rd/24th century and Earth belongs to a federation of planets not unlike the UN. Usually Earth is at war with the Klingons, although there are also successful attempts to live at peace (esp. under *Chancellor Gorkon*). The Klingon nation is a warrior society based on pride, tradition, honour and aggressiveness. It is permanently at war and death in battle is the greatest honour a Klingon can achieve. Consequently Klingons actively seek confrontations. An assassination is an honourable act, as long as the assassin shows his face to the victim and kills at close quarters. To kill an individual from behind or with poison is considered dishonourable. Of course Klingons have their own language and a Klingon edition of *Hamlet* exists.

- Read the two soliloquies mentioned in the text:
- Find out in which situations Hamlet delivers these speeches. Which one do you find more convincing? Why?

At a state banquet the Klingon chancellor Gorkon, who wants to negotiate a peace treaty with the federation, cites the second part of the TO BE OR NOT TO BE soliloquy:

- What answer would you give Spock?
- Fill in the missing words in Gorkon's answer:

| undeclared war · war, battle (*one gap*) · peace metaphor · fear · destroy · unknown · honor and glory |

'But do you not see that it is a _____ concerning fear of the _____ ? Our people have been in what amounts to a state of _____ with your Federation for nearly seven decades – and why? Because _____ is all we know. Because _____ is something new, different, frightening us. But we must be willing to embrace the _____ and move forward into what awaits us. Into the future. We must find a way to reconcile our warrior concept of _____ with the concept of peaceful coexistence with other cultures. Otherwise [...] we will _____ ourselves.'

J.M. Dillard, *Star Trek II – The Undiscovered Country*, p. 78 f.

☀ ☀ ☀ ☀ WHATEVER

1 Shakespeare's lifetime?

| **A** 1558–1610 | **T** 1564–1616 | **D** 1588–1624 | **E** 1590–1648 |

2 Where was he born?

| **S** London | **W** Southwark | **Y** Hampstead | **H** Stratford |

3 Was his father

| **C** a baker? | **K** a teacher? | **O** an alderman? | **L** a poet? |

4 Which foreign language(s) did he learn at school?

| **M** French | **U** Latin and Greek | **N** Spanish | **Z** Italian |

5 How old were Shakespeare and Anne Hathaway when they married?

| **X** 21 and 19 | **W** 25 and 27 | **M** 18 and 26 | **F** 24 and 21 |

6 How many children did they have?

| **H** No children | **J** A boy and a girl | **A** A girl and twins | **G** A girl |

7 What was the name of the players' company Shakespeare joined in London?

| **A** The Queens Men | **Y** The Lord Chamberlaines Men | **D** The Earl's Company | **X** Blackfriars |

8 Who was his patron?

| **S** The Earl of Southampton | **B** Queen Elizabeth | **K** The Earl of Essex | **N** The Mayor of London |

9 How many plays did he write?

| **K** 37 | **T** 24 | **R** 16 | **B** 41 |

10 What kinds of plays did he write?

| **U** Popular plays of domestic life | **F** Comedies and sketches | **V** Miracle plays and moralities | **H** Tragedies, comedies, histories and romances |

11 Macbeth is

| **W** a comedy? | **X** an historical play? | **W** a romance? | **A** a tragedy? |

YOU WILL ☀ ☀ ☀ ☀

12 A Midsummer Night's Dream is

| M | a comedy? | V | a romance? | R | an historical play? | T | a tragedy? |

13 How many sonnets did Shakespeare write?

| W | 34 | B | 9 | P | 132 | E | 154 |

14 Which of these theatres was Shakespeare a co-owner of?

| R | The Swan | F | The Rose | T | The Globe | M | The Theatre |

15 What was Shakespeare's audience like?

| I | Educated | A | Noble | H | Every social class | F | Common people |

16 The role of a woman was played by

| B | a man? | G | a woman? | Y | a boy? | W | a girl? |

17 Where is Shakespeare buried?

| P | In Westminster Abbey, London | U | In St Paul's Cathedral, London | W | In Holy Trinity Church, Stratford-upon-Avon | S | At an unknown place |

18 'West Side Story' is a modern version of Shakespeare's

| D | Antony and Cleopatra | M | Love's Labour's Lost | R | The Comedy of Errors | I | Romeo and Juliet |

19 The film 'Shakespeare in Love' refers to the play

| Y | Love Labour's Lost | L | Romeo and Juliet | F | The Merry Wives of Windsor | Z | As You Like It |

20 Which Shakespeare play did Rita in Russell's 'Educating Rita' watch?

| O | Hamlet? | P | King Lear? | N | Henry V? | L | Macbeth? |

- *The right letters put in a line make a quotation from one of Shakespeare's sonnets:*

| | | | | | | | | | | | | | | | | | | | | | |

Now try to make your own Shakespeare Quiz.

Teacher's Notes

Um die Arbeit in der Oberstufe vorzubereiten, hat es sich als sinnvoll erwiesen, hin und wieder schon in der Mittelstufe einen Exkurs zu Shakespeare einzuschieben. Deshalb sind viele der angebotenen Worksheets variabel einsetzbar und nicht nur für die Oberstufe geeignet. Das Angebot versteht sich als Kaleidoskop, als „Wühlkiste", nicht als Einführungskurs.

Die Film-Zeitangaben beziehen sich jeweils auf das Video, nicht auf die DVD. Beginn ist das erste Bild des Films.

8
William Who?

Hier bietet sich Gruppenarbeit an, dann wäre eine Kopie des biografischen Materials pro Gruppe ausreichend. Den Fragebogen erhalten alle S.

Last name: Shakespeare
First name: William
Place of birth: Henley Street (street); Stratford-upon-Avon (town), Warwickshire (county), England (country)
Date of birth: 23.4.1564
Mother: Mary Arden
Mother's family: rich farmers
Father: John Shakespeare
Father's profession: local politician and businessman
School: Stratford grammar school
Marriage: at age 18 to Ann Hathaway, age 26, on 28.11.1582
Possible reason for marriage: Ann was expecting a baby
Children: Susanna, May 1583, Hamnet and Judith, 2.2.1585
Place of residence from 1585 – 1594: no information
Place of residence in 1594: London
Profession from 1594 on: actor and writer
Coat of arms: bought in 1596 by William for his father to make the family look nobler
Additional profession in 1599: co-owner of theatre 'The Globe'
Financial situation in later life: quite good
Date of death: 23.4.1616
Grave: Holy Trinity Church in Stratford-upon Avon

10 – 13
On the Shakespeare Trail

Sie können das Spiel auch zu einem flexiblen Klassenspiel umfunktionieren und es auf die aktuelle Unterrichtssituation beziehen:

Nach Abschluss einer Unterrichtseinheit teilt die Klasse gemeinsam mit L den behandelten Stoff in drei Themenbereiche auf (z.B. *life, works in general, Hamlet in particular* ...). Die S werden aufgefordert, zu Hause die ganze Einheit durchzugehen und auf DIN A 7-Karten eine bestimmte Anzahl von Fragen zu jedem Themenblock zu notieren: Auf der Vorderseite steht jeweils eine Frage, auf der Rückseite die Antwort.

Die Fragekarten werden eingesammelt und auf Fehler und Beantwortbarkeit geprüft. In der nächsten Stunde erhält jede Gruppe einen Spielplan, Spielsteine, Würfel und ca. 24 Karten (je nach Größe der Gruppen und Anzahl der Themenbereiche) aus den nach Themenbereichen getrennt sortierten Stapeln.

Ca. 15 – 20 Felder auf dem Spielplan werden mit verschiedenen Symbolen (🎭)(♡)(😊) (so viele wie Themenblöcke, von den S erfinden lassen) gekennzeichnet. Auf diesen Feldern muss eine entsprechende Frage beantwortet werden. Ist sie richtig beantwortet, darf der Spieler die Karte behalten, bei einer falschen Antwort kommt sie zurück in den Stapel.

Das Spiel ist zu Ende, wenn jeder Spieler mindestens eine Fragenkarte zu jedem Thema besitzt. Gewonnen hat, wer dann, wenn der letzte Spieler seine dritte Karte erhält, die meisten Karten hat.

14/15
My Shakespeare, Your Shakespeare

Die Bilder werden ausgeschnitten und mithilfe der Zahlen in die richtige Reihenfolge gebracht. Dann können die Bildunterschriften den Zeitangaben nach zugeordnet werden. Als Lösungswort ergibt sich SHAKESPEARE. Am Shakespeare-ähnlichsten sind wohl das Chandos-Portrait und die Skulptur am Grab, da sie zu Lebzeiten bzw. kurz danach angefertigt wurden und noch von Zeitgenossen beurteilt wurden.

Timeline:
S Chandos portrait, late 16th century (1)
H Sculpture near Shakespeare's grave, 1616 (2)
A Engraving by Droeshout, 1623 (3)
K Painting by Gerard Soest, 1681 (4)
E Picture from a collection of Shakespeare's works, 19th century (5)
S Drawing by Picasso, 1964 (6)
P Cover of a book that sees Shakespeare in a new light (cf. glasses!), 1990 (7)
E Children's painting, late 20th century (8)
A Advertisement for the BBC radio, 1998 (9)
R Student's sketch, 2001 (10)
E Shakespeare as a man from another planet (cf. *The Universal Shakespeare*, S. 70 f.), 23rd century (11)

Bart und Haartracht bleiben meist gleich, ansonsten wird das Portrait (wie auch das Werk) der Zeit entsprechend interpretiert. *Shacosper, Shakestaff* ...: Es sind 83 verschiedene Schreibungen des Familiennamens *Shakespeare* überliefert.

16/17
A Player's Day

Dawn:	*Wake up and learn part*
8 am:	*get up and run to the theatre*

8.15 am:	*have to play the part of Ben, too*
9 am:	*rehearsing 'Two Gentlemen of Verona'*
11.30 am:	*get pies and ale for everyone*
12 noon:	*eat and listen to new play*
2 pm:	*dressing for afternoon performance*
2.30 pm:	*afternoon performance*
5.30 pm:	*afternoon performance is over, preparing for private evening performance*
6.30 pm:	*setting off for evening performance*
10.30 pm:	*go to bed*

Eating and sleeping: ca. 10 hours
Leisure time activities: werden nicht ausdrücklich genannt und finden nur an freien Tagen statt
Work in the theatre: ca. 8 hours
Work outside the theatre: ca. 6 hours
(Vorstellungen außer Haus, Rollenlernen)

Die Zahlen können nur sehr ungefähr errechnet werden, sie können und sollen natürlich diskutiert werden. Außer dem Mittagessen bleiben alle Mahlzeiten unerwähnt! Besonders deutlich werden sollen die langen Arbeitszeiten und die Tatsache, dass Freizeit und Privatleben nicht selbstverständlich sind.

18
Globe Theatre

Das Bild zeigt das Innere des *Globe* während einer Vorstellung.

Lösungen: ❶ R ❷ F ❸ S ❹ Q ❺ X ❻ M ❼ T ❽ Y ❾ B

19
Blackfriars

Das Bild zeigt einen Aufriss des *Blackfriar* während einer Vorstellung.

Lösungen: ❶ X ❷ C ❸ N ❹ P ❺ Z ❻ V ❼ E ❽ A ❾ G

20/21
A Day Out in London

Im Gegensatz zu *A Player's Day* (S. 16 f.) werden hier hauptsächlich Freizeitaktivitäten im elisabethanischen England beschrieben. Der Weg des Erzählers kann auf einem Stadtplan mitverfolgt werden. Im Unterrichtsgespräch können verschiedene Informationen ergänzt werden:

cock-fights: fighting cocks or gamecocks have been bred for thousands of years. Cock-fights were very popular, especially in the Roman Empire. Sometimes the cocks were even fitted with metal spurs. Nowadays cock-fights are illegal in GB, Canada and most parts of the US, but are still popular in Asia and former Spanish colonies.

Bull-baiting/bear-baiting: *from the 11th century bull-/bear-baiting became increasingly popular until Shakespeare's times. A bear was chained to a stake, sometimes with its teeth ground down, and four specially bred mastiffs were let loose on it. With bulls the fight was one to one and the chance of a dog being tossed on the bull's horns was considerable. The 'sport' was abolished in 1835.*

Bear baiting ist in England seit dem 11. Jahrhundert belegt und wurde 1835 abgeschafft. *Cock-fights* sind heute in GB verboten, aber noch sehr populär in Asien (z.B. in Indonesien) und in ehemaligen spanischen Kolonien. Die Hähne werden oft mit Metallsporen ausgestattet.

Die S können über ihre Einstellung zum Theater nachdenken. Möchte man das Thema vertiefen, bieten sich WS *Good Night, Sweet Prince* (26/27) und WS *Let Us on Your Imaginary Forces Work* (33) an.

22
Globe-trotting

Sollen die *workshops* praktisch durchgeführt werden, sind einige Requisiten erforderlich. Für die „normale" Bühne werden ein Stück Stoff als Vorhang und einige Lampen (starke Taschenlampen als Ersatz für Scheinwerfer) benötigt. Pappe und Papier für Bühnenbilder und Schilder sind nützlich.
Die tatsächliche *Workshop Season* im neuen Globe fand 1995 statt.

Programme for workshop season: Lighting in a daylight theatre? Acoustics in an open-air theatre? Scenery in a theatre without curtain?

For further information:
www.shakespeare-globe.org
www.rdg.ac.uk/globe
www.shakespeare-gesellschaft.de
http://dreigutelinks.de/literatur/shakespeare.htm

23
A Beaker for Mr Marlowe
Shakespeare in Love 0.18.00

The sequence begins with the dialogue between the playwrights William Shakespeare and Christopher (Kit) Marlowe in an alehouse. It ends after their talk:

Marlowe:	Give my friend a beaker of your best brandy.
Shakespeare:	Kit.
Marlowe:	How goes it, Will?
Shakespeare:	Wonderful. Wonderful.
Marlowe:	Burbage says you have a play.
Shakespeare:	I have, and the chinks to show for it. I insist, a beaker for Mr. Marlowe. I hear you have a new play for The Curtain.
Marlowe:	Not new, my Dr. Faustus.
Shakespeare:	I love your early work: 'Is this the face that launched a thousand ships, and burnt the topless towers of Illium?'

Marlowe:	I have a new one nearly finished, and better: The Massacre at Paris.
Shakespeare:	Good title.
Marlowe:	Yours?
Shakespeare:	Romeo and Ethel the Pirate's Daughter. Yes, I know, I know.
Marlowe:	What is the story?
Shakespeare:	Well, there's this pirate ... in truth I haven't written a word.
Marlowe:	Romeo, Romeo is Italian, always in and out of love.
Shakespeare:	Yes, that's good. Until he meets ...
Marlowe:	Ethel.
Shakespeare:	Do you think?
Marlowe:	The daughter of his enemy.
Shakespeare:	The daughter of his enemy.
Marlowe:	His best friend is killed in a duel by Ethel's brother, or something. His name is Mercutio.
Shakespeare:	Mercutio, good name. Good luck with yours, Kit.
Marlowe:	I thought your play was for Burbage.
Shakespeare:	This is a different one.
Marlowe:	A different one you haven't written?

Pairwork 2: Vor dem Betrachten des Videoausschnittes versetzen sich die S in die Rolle des Filmregisseurs und erstellen Aufzeichnungen zu Requisiten, Handlungsorten und deren Ausstattung, zur Handlung, Mimik und Gestik, zu den Haupt- und Nebendarstellern, der Stimmung und Tonlage sowie der nichtsprachlichen Kommunikation.

Die Notizen münden in einen ersten Versuch der Partner, die Szene aufzuführen, so wie sie sie sich vorstellen.

Alternativ können S, die den Filmausschnitt bereits gesehen haben, Mitschüler, die die Szene noch nicht kennen, mit ganz konkreten und sprachlich präzisen Anweisungen anleiten, die Szene aufzuführen. Ziel ist es, so eng wie möglich an die Originalvorlage heranzukommen. Die gemeinsame Betrachtung der Szene kann am Ende der Teamarbeit zur Kontrolle dienen.

Zu seiner Zeit war Shakespeare übrigens keineswegs so einzigartig und herausragend, wie er später oft dargestellt wurde. Es gab andere Erfolgsautoren, die damals evtl. bekannter und beliebter waren. Zu ihnen zählt Christopher Marlowe (*Tamburlain, The Jew of Malta, Doctor Faustus* u. a.), der mit erst 29 Jahren in einer Kneipe ermordet wurde.

24
A Royal Discussion
Shakespeare in Love 0.58

The sequence begins when Viola enters the palace at Greenwich. It ends after the exchange with Queen Elizabeth I.

Viola is invited to attend a celebration in Greenwich. She meets Queen Elizabeth I. who

among other issues discusses the merits and benefits of theatre and poetry with her. The queen has a rather down-to-earth view on this matter, whereas Viola is very enthusiastic, particularly about her favourite playwright William Shakespeare.
The discussion does not get very far because there are so many other people present and other matters to attend to.

25
The Queen's Glove

Richtige Szenenfolge: ① Szene 3, ② Szene 1, ③ Szene 5, ④ Szene 2, ⑤ Szene 4

26/27
Good Night, Sweet Prince

This is what Elizabethan writers came up with: elaborate costumes, a lot of action and fights on stage, very expressive mime, pantomime, comical scenes (dumb shows), frequent change between action-packed and slow-motion scenes, special effects (lowering actors on stage from above, trap doors to let actors appear from below, etc.).

28/29
Steal Hamlet

Dieser Auszug aus einem Jugendbuch spiegelt die Situation der Bühnenautoren zu Shakespeares Zeit wider. Es gab kein Copyright in unserem Sinn und der Text eines neuen Stückes war ein gut gehütetes Geheimnis. Ungewöhnlich war die Herausgabe einer Sammlung von Shakespeares Stücken mit autorisierten Texten nach dessen Tod (*First Folio*), die die Flut von schlechten Mitschriften (*Bad Quartos*) eindämmen sollte. (*Folio* und *Quarto* bezeichnen die Größe der bedruckten Seite.)
Der *First Folio*-Text ist im *Bad Quarto* kaum mehr zu erkennen. Am leichtesten sind noch die Zeilen 1/1 und 9/2 zu identifizieren.

30
Will's Works

Waagerecht: *Winter's Tale, King Lear, Othello, Julius Caesar* (auch von rechts nach links)
Senkrecht: *Hamlet, Tempest*
Über Eck oder verteilt: *Twelfth Night, Romeo and Juliet, Love's Labour's Lost, Merchant of Venice, Merry Wives of Windsor, Troilus and Cressida*
Es gibt keine „diagonalen" Lösungswörter, jedoch einige weitere, unvollständige Werke-Titel.

31
The Essential Shakespeare

Diese Methode einer graphischen Zusammenfassung der Stücke ist gut in allen Jahrgangsstufen (mit steigender Komplexität) einzusetzen. In der Unterstufe und in der Mittelstufe kann ein Stück, das vorher in einer einfachen, inhaltsorientierten Fassung auf Englisch oder Deutsch vorgestellt wurde, so als Poster festgehalten werden. In der Oberstufe kann sich die Klasse schnell in Partnerarbeit einen Überblick über das Gesamtwerk verschaffen, wenn die in den Gruppen erarbeiteten Stücke dem Plenum vorgestellt werden.

32
What Joy is Joy?
Shakespeare in Love 0.19.30 and 0.12.00

The sequence (0.19.30) begins with an audition in the theatre. The first four actors we can see and hear do not exactly leave a lasting impression. Will Shakespeare is frustrated and disappointed and lies down on a bench when Thomas Kent enters. Kent is Viola de Lesseps in disguise. She beautifully recites Valentine's monologue from The Two Gentlemen of Verona *(Act III, Scene 1).*

Spielen Sie den Anfang dieser Szene und zeigen Sie den S die Auftritte der ersten drei Möchtegern-Schauspieler. Halten Sie aber das Band an, bevor Viola de Lesseps die Bühne betritt.

Geben sie der Klasse den Text, den Viola vortragen wird. Lassen Sie die S den Monolog einüben, wobei sie verschiedene Möglichkeiten des Sprechens erproben (z.B. still und leise, leidenschaftltich, arrogant, traurig, wutentbrannt usw.). Geben sie ihnen Gelegenheit, ihre Versionen der Klasse vorzutragen. Zeigen Sie dann den Rest der Videosequenz, damit die S nun ihre Form der Darbietung mit der von Viola de Lesseps alias Thomas Kent vergleichen können.

Der selbe Monolog findet sich auch am Anfang des Films (0.12.00). Dort kann man ihn bei einer Burbage-Aufführung für die Königin in Whitehall hören. Es ist höchst interessant, die Reaktion der Königin auf den Text mit der Violas zu vergleichen. Während Elizabeth gelangweilt scheint, kennt Viola den Monolog offensichtlich auswendig. Sie sitzt mit geschlossenen Augen, ist zutiefst bewegt, sie spricht den Text leise mit.

Als Schlussaufgabe bietet es sich an, die S ein eigenes Gedicht schreiben zu lassen. Sie können dabei der Shakespeare-Vorlage mit dem Muster der rhetorischen Frage und den sich anschließenden Antworten folgen.

33
Let Us on Your Imaginary Forces Work

Outback theatre: relies on interesting play, well-trained actors, exciting dialogues; imagery is created with the help of words.
Film: all details of an action can realistically be filmed, special effects and elaborate set-ups are used to create a scene.

34 – 37
Henry V – Killer or Hero

Branagh's questions – Charles' answers

① *'Prince Charles concurred: Yes, there was a tremendous pressure and temptation to be at times either very silly or very violent. As with most people, these impulses were resisted but the underlying pressure was greater than most*

people would ever experience.'
② *'I asked Prince Charles whether the various newspaper betrayals of events, dramatic and mundane, had changed him. Yes, it had, profoundly. And it had, as I suspected was true of Henry, produced an extraordinary melancholy. It was a sadness that could either produce bitterness or a more useful but painful wisdom, [...]'*
③ *'[...] Prince Charles was in total agreement. Some kind of belief in God was the only practical way of living from day to day, it was the only way to deal with his position.'*

Evidence in the play (Branagh's interpretation)

→ ① *'In Henry this meant (as has been proven by many productions) that the sense of humour which I felt belonged to the man was often missing, as was his latent violence, in fact all the extremes of human behaviour which in ordinary mortals find their own balance but which in a pressurised monarch could emerge with even greater force.'*
→ ② *'Henry makes one attempt in the play to be like other men. During the famous night-time sequence he walks among his men in disguise. The experience is extremely unsatisfactory: he wants to be one of them, but he can't be; he wants them to understand his position but they resist it.'*
→ ③ *'There is little solace to be found in remoteness. I believed that Henry's only real comfort could be his faith, [...]'*
Quotes from: Kenneth Branagh: *Beginning.* Pan Books: London, 1990, p. 142 ff

38 – 40
Hamlet: A Ghostly Interview

Der hier abgedruckte Text ist eine für die Mittelstufe gekürzte Version von Akt 1, Szenen 1, 4 und 5.Sie kann ohne großen Aufwand aus jeder beliebigen Hamlet-Tonaufnahme zusammenkopiert werden. Der Text beginnt bei Szene 1, Zeilen 33 – 55; es folgen Szene 4, Zeilen 1 – 6; 38 – 45, 57 – 68, dann Szene 5, Zeilen 1 – 28.

Bernardo describes *the position of a star.*
Horatio should speak to the ghost because *he is an educated man.*
Horatio wants to know *who the ghost is that looks like the dead king of Denmark.*
He wants the ghost to *say something* but the ghost *walks away.*
Weather: *cold with a biting wind.*
Time: *just about midnight.*
What should happen at that time? *The ghost should appear.*
Hamlet wonders whether the ghost *is a good or a bad ghost.*
The ghost tells Hamlet to come with him because *he wants to speak to Hamlet alone.*
Hamlet is not afraid because *he believes his soul will live forever.*
Hamlet wants to know *where the ghost is going.*
The ghost asks Hamlet to *listen to him.*
Very soon the ghost will have to go *to purgatory and pay for his sins in never ending*

flames.
The ghost must not *tell anybody what it is like where he is.*
What would happen if he did? *Hamlet would be terrified.*
The ghost wants Hamlet to *listen to his story of murder* and then *to kill his murderer.*

The ghost's story: The ghost is Hamlet's father. He has to suffer in the flames of hell during the day and walk around as a ghost during the night. He has to do that until all his sins (and sins related to him) are paid for.

41
Bitten by a Snake

Besonders in der Mittelstufe führt der Ansatz, Hamlet als Krimi zu behandeln, noch zu echten Diskussionen. Die Auflösung bringt die Inhaltsangabe auf WS 42/43.

42/43
Murder Most Foul, Strange and Unnatural

Die Texte können einfach nur gemeinsam als Zusammenfassung gelesen und/oder in Gruppenarbeit stückweise bearbeitet werden.

The rest is: **S I L E N C E**

44
To Do it or not to Do it
or: the making of a decision

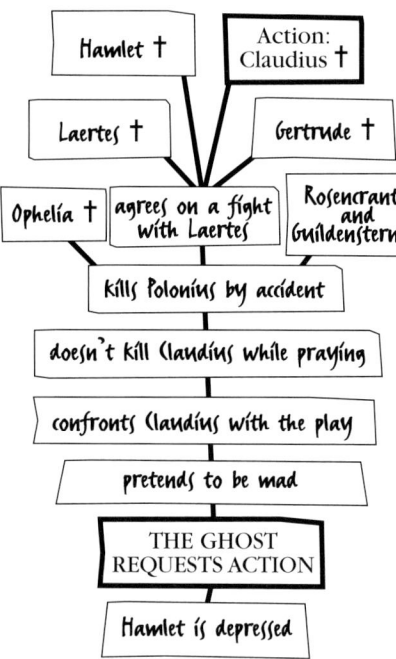

Why did the action take so long?
→ *melancholic disposition*
→ *shock (father dead, mother married)*
→ *wants to check evidence first*
→ *waits for a good moment*
→ *doesn't want to hurt Gertrude*
→ *would become guilty himself*

47
Is this a Dagger …
Dead Poets Society 0.39

The sequence begins with Keating talking to his

class at school. First he discusses language with the students, then he talks about ways of reciting Shakespeare. He imitates different people: a classical British actor, Laurence Olivier in Richard III, a nasal Marlon Brando and a rugged John Wayne: "Is this a dagger I see before me?" is a line from Macbeth's famous soliloquy in Macbeth, Act II, Scene 1.

Spielen Sie die Videosequenz, in der Keating über Shakespeare spricht. Geben Sie dann der Klasse den Text des Monologs. Bitten Sie die S, ihn auszuprobieren und einzuüben. Dabei sollen sie verschiedene Arten des Sprechens, Möglichkeiten der Präsentation und angestrebte Wirkungen erfahren.
Die S erhalten Gelegenheit, ihre Entwürfe vorzutragen und miteinander zu vergleichen.

48 – 51
The Tempest

Die Randfiguren bieten Gelegenheit über die Rolle der *groundlings* zu sprechen (vgl. auch: S. 20 f).

52
There is a Scene Missing
Shakespeare in Love 1.13

The sequence begins when Will starts speaking to the cast and ends with Ned mentioning marriage and death.

In this part of the video Shakespeare explains the end of his play Romeo and Juliet. *Everybody on the stage is moved until one of the actors notices that 'there is a scene missing between marriage and death'.*

Die S werden zunächst aufgefordert, sich in dieser *information gap exercise* vorzustellen, was der Filmausschnitt enthalten könnte.

Spielen Sie ihn der Klasse vom Band vor. Bitten Sie die S, die WS zu bearbeiten und ihre Egebnisse zu präsentieren.

Spielen Sie mindestens die nächste Sequenz, wenn möglich auch noch die folgende. Sie beinhalten exakt die Szene, die gefehlt hatte und die jetzt von Will Shakespeare und Viola de Lesseps gespielt wird. Im Drama ist Juliets Zimmer der Handlungsort, im Film beginnt die Szene in Violas Zimmer und wird im Theater fortgeführt, wo die beiden allein sind und beginnen sich zu lieben.

(Die Videoversion des Films ist für Jugendliche ab 15 Jahren geeignet).

It is interesting to note that Juliet's part in the original drama is spoken by Will; in the film Viola speaks Romeo's part.

Will: Wilt thou be gone? It is not yet near day:
It was the nightingale, and not the lark,
That pierc'd the fearful hollow of thine ear;
Nightly she sings on yon pomegranate tree:

Believe me, love, it was the nightingale.

Viola: It was the lark, the herald of the morn,
No nightingale: look, love, what envious streaks
Do lace the severing clouds in yonder east:
Night's candles are burnt out, and jocund day
Stands tiptoe on the misty mountain tops:
I must be gone and live, or stay and die.

The continuation of the scene is spoken in the theatre while the protagonists are undressing each other:

Will: Yon light is not daylight, I know it, I:
It is some meteor that the sun exhales,
To be to thee this night a torch-bearer,
And light thee on thy way to Mantua:
Therefore stay yet; thou need'st not to be gone,

Viola: Let me ta'en, let me be put to death;
I am content, so thou wilt have it so,
I'll say yon grey is not the morning's eye …

I have more care to stay than will to go:
Come, death, and welcome! Juliet willst it so.

Romeo and Juliet, Act III, Scene 5

Fragen Sie Ihre S: *Imagine what the scene will look like on stage during the theatre performance.*

53
Shakespeare in Love
Shakespeare in Love 0.28

The first part of the sequence begins when Shakespeare approaches Viola de Lesseps' house through the garden after a dance.
It ends immediately as he begins to climb a plant next to the balcony.

Zeigen Sie auf gar keinen Fall, wie Shakespeare die Balustrade des Balkons erreicht!

Lassen Sie die Schritte 1 bis 4 bearbeiten.

Zeigen Sie nach dem vierten Arbeitsschritt den zweiten Teil des Videoausschnittes. Shakespeare klettert auf den Balkon und schaut über das Geländer. Der Überraschungsmoment ist erreicht, wenn die S erkennen, dass es gar keine richtige Fortsetzung des Dialogs auf dem Balkon geben wird. Ganz unerwartet findet sich Shakespeare beim Erklimmen der Balustrade Auge in Auge mit Violas *nurse*. Beide sind so überrascht, dass sie laut aufschreien. Die Amme läuft weg. Shakespeare fällt in den Garten und kommt rücklings in einem akkurat geschnittenen Busch zu liegen. Die Wächter verfolgen Will in einer wilden Verfolgungsjagd durch den Park.

Da ein Gespräch nicht einmal im Ansatz entsteht, ist diese Szene eine herrliche Parodie auf die berühmte Balkonszene in *Romeo and Juliet*.

55
'Sugared' Sonnets

In 1598 Shakespeare's sonnets had not yet been published and were only passed on among friends and read in private. Frances Meres, a headmaster and lover of poetry, wrote about them in the same year: "… the sweeete wittie soule of Ouid lives in mellifluous hony-tongued Shakespeare, witnes his Venus and Adnonis, his Lucrece, his sugred Sonnets among private friends, & c." (quoted in: F.E. Halliday: *Shakespeare and his Critics.* Duckworth: London, 1949, p. 21).

Es gibt mehr Wörter zur Auswahl als benötigt werden.
Bei *Sugared Sonnets* sind zu ergänzen (der Reihe nach): *Lovely, temperate, rough, short, hot, gold, changing, eternal, breathe, life.*

56
What's a Sonnet?

Sonnet 130
My mistress' eyes are nothing like the sun;
Coral is far more red than her lips' red;
If snow be white, why then her breasts are dun;
If hairs be wires, black wires grow on her head.
I have seen roses damask'd, red and white,
But no such roses see I in her cheeks;
And in some perfumes is there more delight
Than in the breath that from my mistress reeks;
I love to hear her speak, yet well I know
That music hath a far more pleasing sound;
I grant I never saw a goddess go –
My mistress when she walks treads on the ground.
   And yet, by heaven, I think my love as rare
   As any she belied with false compare.

Sonnet 130 is part of a series of sonnets adressed to an ominous 'dark lady'. Scholars still argue about who Shakespeare might have had in mind when writing this series, but he must have hated and loved her at the same time. It is an anti-Petrarchian sonnet in which all the characteristics commonly attributed by other Elizabethan poets to their ladies are reversed.
→ cf. Kopiervorlage S. 79.

Bei Interesse kann ein Beispiel zum italienischen Sonett besprochen werden.

The Italian or Petrarchan sonnet is divided into an octave (the first 8 lines) and a sestet (the last 6 lines), generally corresponding to the development of the thought: the statement of a general idea in the octave followed by a specific example in the sestet. Famous English poets such as Milton, Wordsworth and Keats have written notable sonnets in the Italian form.
→ cf. Kopiervorlage S. 79.

Strophe 1: *by/majesty:* Hier handelt es sich um einen *visual rhyme.*

Composed upon Westminster Bridge
September 3, 1802

Earth has not anything to show more fair: **A**
Dull would he be of soul who could pas by **B**
A sight so touching in its majesty: **B**
This City now doth, like a garment, wear **A**

The beauty of the morning; silent, bare, **A**
Ships towers, domes, theatres,
and temples lie **B**
Open unto the fields, and so the sky; **B**
All bright and glittering in the
smokeless air. **A**

Never did sun more beautifully steep. **G**
In his first splendour, valley, rock, or hill; **D**
Ne'er saw I, never felt, a calm so deep! **E**

The river glideth at his own sweet will: **G**
Dear God! the very houses seem asleep; **D**
And all that mighty heart is lying still! **E**

William Wordsworth

57/58
Listen to Your Heart Beat

Beim Einsatz in der Mittelstufe hat es sich bewährt, zu einem frühen Zeitpunkt eine Video-Fassung der Rede Henrys hinzuzuziehen. Empfehlenswert ist die Spielfilm-Version von Kenneth Branagh.
The Henry Speech uses mainly enjambement to break the monotony of the rhythm. The Hamlet lines are an heroic couplet and are consequently to be found at the end of the scene.

61/62
Thou Puking Boil-brained Horn-beast

Elizabethan English wird z.B. in den USA auf sog. *Elizabethan faires* (eine Art lebendes Museum/Themenpark) gesprochen, wo die Akteure sich der Zeit entsprechend kleiden und auch Schnellkurse in elizabethanischem Englisch machen können.
Zwei der „Mäntel" enthalten Adjektive, einer Nomen. Es werden immer zwei Adjektive mit einem Nomen verknüpft.

Lösung Puzzle:

The Queen | Sir Master Mistress
Your Grace Your Highness | Well dressed person, but not nobility
My lord My lady | Sirrah/Wench
Nobleman Noblewoman | Serving man Serving woman

63–65
Acting

Using your voice: Die S sollen ausprobieren, wie Stimme, Intonation, Pausen etc. einen Text zur Wirkung bringen.

Ausschnitte aus: einer Sportreportage, *Macbeth* (Act IV, Scene 1), Kind wird in den Schlaf gewiegt, auf dem Kasernenhof.

Acting is ... using your body

Das Gesten-Alphabet:
A: Ich gebe Geld
B: Ich helfe dir
C: Ich bin wütend
D: Ich habe keinen Beweis/ich weiß nicht
E: Ich bestrafe
F: Ich schlage
G: Ich vertraue
H: Ich hindere
I: Ich rate
K: Ich führe dich
L: Ich bin ungeduldig
M: Ich denke nach
N: Ich schäme mich
O: Ich bewundere dich.
P: Ich bestätige gewissenhaft
Q: Ich zeige Reue
R: Ich fürchte Entrüstung
S: Ich verspreche feierlich
T: Wir versöhnen uns
V: Ich bin misstrauisch
W: Ich ehre dich
X: Ich grüße mit Zurückhaltung
Y: Ich bin aufgeregt/wütend
Z: Ich segne dich

Ralph Richardson is an actor colleague of Laurence Olivier.

68
Reinvention of Winter

Winter.
When icicles hang by the wall,
And Dick the shepherd blows his nail,
And Tom bears logs into the hall,
And milk comes frozen home in pail,
When blood is nipp'd, and ways be foul,
Then nightly sings the staring owl:
'Tu-who;
Tu-whit, Tu-who' - A merry note,
While greasy Joan doth keel the pot.

When all aloud the wind doth blow,
And coughing drowns the parson's saw,
And birds sit brooding in the snow,
And Marian's nose looks red and raw,
When roasted crabs hiss in the bowl,
Then nightly sings the staring owl:
'Tu-who;
Tu-Whit, To-who' - A merry note,
While greasy Joan doth keel the pot.

From: Love's Labour's Lost, Act 5, Scene 2

69
Shakespeare and Myself

Der Text soll die S zur Reflektion über Shakespeare anregen, nachdem sie bereits einiges von ihm besprochen / über ihn gehört haben.
Es bietet sich ein Gespräch an über *bardolatry* und den automatischen Respekt, der Shakespeare als „schwierigem" Autor oft entgegengebracht wird. Die S sollen ermutigt werden, ihren eigenen Zugang zu Shakespeare zu suchen und zu finden.

70
The Universal Shakespeare

Der Perspektivenwechsel zu Shakespeare in der Zukunft soll die nötige Distanz schaffen, einen neuen Blick auf Hamlet zu werfen und aus alten Interpretationsmustern auszubrechen.

Quellenangaben zu den genannten Videos:
CIC Video, Paramount: *Star Trek VI: The Undiscovered Country*, 1991
CIC Video, Paramount: *Star Trek, The Next Generation*, Cassette 29 (*The Vengeance Factor & The Defector*)
CIC Video, Paramount: *Star Trek, The Next Generation*, Cassette 88 (*Emergence & Preemptive Strike*)

The Klingon language has been invented by linguist Marc Okrand to go with the Star Trek *feature films and TV series and went off to have a life of its own. Star Trek fans started to learn 'the fastest growing language in the universe', a language institute was founded which offers language courses and a platform for translation projects such as the Bible or Shakespeare's works. Further information:* www.kli.org *or Klingon Language Institute, P.O. Box 643, 19031 Flourtown, PA.*

Lückentext: *metaphor • unknown • undeclared war • war, battle • fear • peace • honor and glory • destroy*

Video: der Kinofilm *Star Trek VI: The Undiscovered Country*.
Auch einige Serienfolgen bieten brauchbares Material für den Shakespeare-Unterricht, besonders in der Staffel *Star Trek – The Next Generation*, da hier der Kapitän des Raumschiffes, Captain Picard, erklärter Shakespeare-Bewunderer ist und das Thema immer wieder aufgreift. Besonders ergiebig sind: *The Defector* (*The Next Generation*, 3. Saison) mit Parallelen zu *Henry V* und *Emergence* (*The Next Generation*, 7. Saison) mit Anspielungen auf *The Tempest*.

72
Whatever You Will

THOU MAYST HAVE THY WILL
From: *Sonnet 143*

Sonnet 130

My mistress' eyes are nothing like the sun;
Coral is far more red than her lips' red;
If snow be white, why then her breasts are dun;
If hairs be wires, black wires grow on her head.
I have seen roses damask'd, red and white,
But no such roses see I in her cheeks;
And in some perfumes is there more delight
Than in the breath that from my mistress reeks;
I love to hear her speak, yet well I know
That music hath a far more pleasing sound;
I grant I never saw a goddess go –
My mistress when she walks treads on the ground.
   And yet, by heaven, I think my love as rare
   As any she belied with false compare.

Composed upon Westminster Bridge
September 3, 1802

Earth has not anything to show more fair:
Dull would he be of soul who could pas by
A sight so touching in its majesty:
This City now doth, like a garment, wear

The beauty of the morning; silent, bare,
Ships towers, domes, theatres,
and temples lie
Open unto the fields, and so the sky;
All bright and glittering in the
smokeless air.

Never did sun more beautifully steep.
In his first splendour, valley, rock, or hill;
Ne'er saw I, never felt, a calm so deep!

The river glideth at his own sweet will:
Dear God! the very houses seem asleep;
And all that mighty heart is lying still!

William Wordsworth

Texts and texts with illustrations

A Player's Day, pp. 16–17: From *Shakespeare's Theatre* by Jacqueline Morley and John James, Simon & Schuster, Hemel Hempstead, Herts., 1994, © The Salariya Book Co. Ltd., Brighton, UK. Used by permission.

A Beaker for Mr Marlowe, pp. 23, 75/ *A Royal Discussion*, p. 24/ *There is a Scene Missing ...*, pp. 52, 77/ *Shakespeare in Love*, p. 53: From film *Shakespeare in Love*, © Universal Studios 1998 and Miramax Film Cooperation.

Steal Hamlet ... or else, pp. 28–29: From *The Shakespeare Stealer* by Gary Blackwood, © 1998 by Gary Blackwood. Used by permissin of Dutton Children's Books, an imprint of Penguin Putnam Books for Young Readers, a division of Penguin Putnam Inc. All rights reserved.

Henry V – Killer or Hero?, pp. 34, 36: From *Beginning* by Kenneth Branagh (Chatto & Windus, 1989), © Kenneth Branagh. Reprinted by permission of The Rod Hall Agency, London, UK.

Shakespeare – Dead Boring?, p. 45/ *Macbeth's a Tragedy, isn't it?*, p. 46: From *Educating Rita* by Willy Russell, © Methuen Publishing Limited, London, UK. Used by permission.

The Tempest, pp. 48–51: From *Mr William Shakespeare's Plays*, © 1998 Marcia Williams. Reproduced by permission of the publisher, Walker Books Ltd., London, UK.

Will's Words, pp. 59–60: From *Pons – Wörterbuch für Schule und Studium*, Ernst Klett Sprachen GmbH, Stuttgart 2001. Used by permission.

Shakespeare and Myself, p. 69: From *How to Be a Yank* by George Mikes (Viking Deutsch, 1992), © 1948 by George Mikes. Reprinted by permission of The Penguin Group (UK).

The Universal Shakespeare, p. 70: From Nick Nicholas, Introduction to: *Hamlet – The Restored Klingon Version*, Flourtown, PA: Klingon Language Institute, 1996.

Illustrations

© Stephen Alcorn, Cambridge, NY/www.alcorngallery.com (original oil painting): p. 29 (top right); Richard Allen: p. 13 (bottom left); Archiv für Kunst und Geschichte GmbH, Berlin: pp. 11 (top left and top right), 12 (second from bottom and bottom), 20 (top), 25 (bottom left); BBC World Service: p. 15 (top left no. 9); Cinetext Bildarchiv, Frankfurt: pp. 5 (top), 23 (top right), 24 (left and right), 32 (bottom), 33 (top right), 45, 47 (all), 52, 53; © Theo Crosby, London: p. 18; © Consignia plc 1995/ Reconstruction of Shakespeare's Globe Stamps. Reproduced by kind permissions of Consignia. All Rights Reserved: pp. 21 (top and second from top), 23 (top left); © Donald Cooper/Shakespeare's Globe, London: p. 27 (middle right); Dpa-Fotoreport: p. 36 (bottom left, © Hertzog; bottom right, © Carsten Rehder); Dpa ZB-Fotoreport: p. 57 (top, © Jens Kalaene); Mary Evans Picture Library, London: pp. 20 (middle left and bottom); Graphiconies (Bortoli): p. 14 (middle left no. 7); Roswitha Hecke, Hamburg: p. 44 (bottom right); © IMSI's MasterPhotos Collection, 1895 Francisco Blvd. East, San Rafael, CA 94901-5506, USA.: p. 63 (top left, middle and bottom); © John James/ The Salariya Book Co. Ltd., Brighton, UK: pp. 19, 21 (bottom), 27 (top left, bottom middle and bottom right); © Richard Kalina/Shakespeare's Globe, London: p. 22 (top and bottom); Klingon Language Institute, Flourtown, PA: p. 71;

©Knife/www.CartoonStock.com: p. 29 (bottom); Holger Lipschütz, Berlin: Introduction (all), pp. 5 (bottom), 6 (top right), 8 (top), 9 (margin), 11 (middle right), 12 (margin), 14 (margin), 19 (margin), 21 (margin), 22 (margin, top right and middle), 23 (bottom), 24 (margin), 25 (right and bottom right), 26 (all), 27 (margin and middle left), 29 (margin), 30 (margin), 31 (all), 32 (margin), 33 (margin and top left), 35 (margin), 38 (margin), 41 (margin and all bottom), 44 (margin), 46 (margin), 55 (margin and bottom), 56 (all), 58 (all), 60 (bottom), 61, 62 (all), 63 (margin and top right), 64 (margin), 66 (all), 67 (all), 68 (margin); Heinz Mahler, Berlin: p. 68; Gabriele Heinisch, Berlin: p. 70 (all); © Succession Picasso/VG Bild-Kunst, Bonn 2002: p. 14 (middle middle no. 6); PWE-Verlag GmbH, Hamburg: pp. 34, 35; RSC-programme: Henry V, 1976: p. 37; The Shakespeare Trust, Stratford-upon-Avon: p. 7 (bottom left); Southwark Cathedral, London: cover; © Gennie Summers 1995/ Klingon Language Institute, Flourtown, PA: p. 14, (middle right no. 11; © Soyuzmultfilm, Moscow 1992/Shakespeare Animated Films Ltd Christmas Joint Venture: pp. 40 (top), 44 (top left); © John Tramper/ Shakespeare's Globe, London: cover, 39 (bottom); © Ross Williamson/ www.CartoonStock.com: p. 54 (bottom).

Sources for images

From *Shakespeare* by Martin Fido, Gallery Press, London 1988, pp. 6 (top left), 8 (middle left, middle right and bottom left), 10 (top left), 12 (third from top), 13 (top left), 14 (top right no. 1), 15 (middle left), 27 (bottom right).

From *The Complete Works of Shakespeare,* The London Printing and Publishing Company, Ltd., o.J.: pp. 14 (bottom right no. 5), 42, 43, 46.

From *Mr. William Shakespeares Comedies, Histories, & Tragedies,* A Facsimile of the First Folio, 1623, Routledge, London 1998: pp. 8 (middle middle), 10 (bottom left), 14 (bottom right no. 5), 28, 30 (bottom middle).